DATE DUE

STOP
TEACHING
OUR KIDS TO KILL

STOP
TEACHING
OUR KIDS
TO KILL

A CALL TO ACTION
AGAINST TV, MOVIE &
VIDEO GAME VIOLENCE

Lt. Col. DAVE GROSSMAN
and GLORIA DEGAETANO

CROWN PUBLISHERS

NEW YORK

Published by Crown Publishers, 201 East 50th Street, New York,
New York 10022. Member of the Crown Publishing Group.

Random House, Inc. New York, Toronto, London, Sydney, Auckland
www.randomhouse.com

CROWN is a trademark and the Crown colophon
is a registered trademark of Random House, Inc.

Manufactured in the United States of America

Design by Leonard Henderson

Library of Congress Cataloging-in-Publication Data
Grossman, Dave.
Stop teaching our kids to kill: a call to action against TV,
movie & video game violence / Dave Grossman,
Gloria DeGaetano.— 1st ed.
Includes bibliographical references and index.
1. Mass media and children.   2. Television and children.
3. Violence on television.   4. Children and violence.
I. DeGaetano, Gloria.   II. Title.
HQ784.M3G76   1999
302.23'083—dc21   99–42476
ISBN 0-609-60613-1

10 9 8 7 6 5 4 3 2 1
First Edition

TO THE CHILDREN OF THE WORLD
AND TO THE SURVIVAL OF THEIR INNOCENCE

ACKNOWLEDGMENTS

It takes a village to make a book! And there are many members of my "village" whom I would like to thank.

First and foremost is my friend and coauthor, Gloria DeGaetano, whose tremendous qualifications, in-depth research, hard work, and positive spirit have made this book possible.

To Doug Pepper, our editor, who has been a friend, coauthor, and fellow believer. To my agent, Richard Curtis, who may have been the very first to truly believe in this book.

To my sainted wife and dearest friend, Jeanne. To Susan Tacker, my assistant and a true gift from above just when we needed her. To my "fairy godmothers" and my "wicked stepsisters," who helped us to make some sense out of the senseless tragedy that struck in Littleton.

To Jack Bowers and Linda Graham and the magnificent group whom I had the privilege to serve beside in Jonesboro after the unthinkable happened there. To my brothers-in-arms and fellow trainers in the law enforcement community. To my tremendously supportive leaders, friends, peers, and students at Arkansas State University.

To my three sons, Jon, Eric, and Joe, who lost a part of their Dad but can turn to the pages of this book, and the fruits thereof, to see where he went. And to Mom and Dad, who taught me to love books and never lost faith, and then had to depart just before I could finish this one.

And to so many others, in the realms of military, peace, academia, medicine, and education, who believed and supported. To all of these I extend my undying thanks and gratitude. May we, together, help to make things just a little better.

—*Lt. Col. Dave Grossman*

This book brewed inside me for over a decade. I am so grateful to Dave Grossman, warrior with heart, for helping pull it out of me. His leadership, passion, and uncompromising standards for making a better world inspire us all!

I am very thankful for the commitment and determination of all the people at Crown. Their dedication to this book juiced up the process and spurred needed energy to meet impossible deadlines. Doug Pepper, senior editor, has my sincere respect and appreciation for all the time, energy, and talent he put in helping us craft a more coherent, incisive manifesto. And, as always, my gratitude continues for Peter Cox, my agent, essential and excellent supporter of my dreams!

Dr. Brandon Centerwall and Dr. Don Shifrin have graciously shared so much of their knowledge over many conversations. They have been not only good buddies throughout the process, but also indispensable experts in keeping us accurate and on track. Thank you so much!

At times writing this book caused the college-type panic when six papers were due immediately. When that happened, friends and family provided comfort and backbone. Pam Bartlett, Lynn Haney, Anna Schwartz, and Wendy Johnson are four powerful women who know how to "nudge and nurture." I am deeply indebted to my wise mother, Ida DeGaetano, for her sage advice and understanding that "chicken did, indeed, come to prove it!" My sister, Barbara, brother, Al, and their families have been a welcome cheering squad. My sons, Matt and Adam, gave me much-needed guidance, heated debates and all. And of course, thanks to my ever-encouraging husband, David Moore, whose intelligent insights and generous spirit are reflected on every page.

—*Gloria DeGaetano*

CONTENTS

STOP
TEACHING
OUR KIDS TO KILL

INTRODUCTION

[The entertainment industry] and the rest of us cannot kid ourselves. Our children are being fed a dependable daily dose of violence—and it sells. Now, thirty years of studies have shown that this desensitizes our children to violence, and to its consequences.

We now know that by the time the typical American child reaches the age of eighteen, he or she has seen 200,000 dramatized acts of violence, and 40,000 dramatized murders. Kids become attracted to it, and more numb to its consequences. As their exposure to violence grows, so, in some deeply troubling cases of particularly vulnerable children, does the taste for it. We should not be surprised that half the video games that a typical seventh-grader plays are violent. . . .

What the studies say, quite simply, is that the boundary between fantasy and reality violence, which is a clear line for most adults, can become very blurred for vulnerable children. Kids steeped in the culture of violence do become desensitized to it and more capable of committing it themselves.

That is why I have strongly urged people in the entertainment industry to consider the consequences of what they create and how they advertise it. One can value the First Amendment right to free speech and at the same time care for and act with restraint.

—*President Bill Clinton, June 1, 1999*

1

OBSERVATIONS FROM JONESBORO, ARKANSAS
BY LT. COL. DAVE GROSSMAN

I am from Jonesboro, Arkansas. I travel the world training medical, law enforcement, and U.S. military personnel about the realities of warfare. I try to make those who carry deadly force keenly aware of the psychological impact of killing. In my various capacities—West Point psychology professor, chair of the Department of Military Science at Arkansas State University, military historian, army ranger—I combine different perspectives to help people understand how to deal with and prevent killing.

So here I am, an expert in the field of "killology," as it is referred to, and a school massacre of terrible proportion happens right in my backyard. (At the time it was the worst such massacre in American history; the events in Littleton, Colorado, just over a year later would claim that awful distinction.) It was March 24, 1998; a schoolyard shooting that left four girls and a teacher dead. Ten others were injured and two boys, ages eleven and thirteen, were convicted of murder.

I spent the first three days after the tragedy at Westside Middle School, where the shootings took place, working with the counselors, teachers, students, and parents. None of us had ever done anything like this before. We all felt that there were lessons to be learned, and perhaps the most important one is this: children do not naturally kill.

A teacher at Westside High School told me about her students' reaction when she went in and told her class that someone had just shot a bunch of middle schoolers. "They laughed," she told me in dismayed amazement. "They laughed." I suppose they may have laughed because they thought the teacher was joking. Or because it was the only, absurd reaction to a truly absurd and horrifying event. But she and I both believed they did so because they have been raised and educated not to take killing seriously. For

2

them violence doesn't hold consequences. Tragically, for many of our kids the loss of human life to violence has become a joke.

There are many explanations for this behavior, but violent entertainment programming is at the top of the list. Children are bombarded with thousands of violent acts on television at a young, vulnerable age when they literally cannot tell the difference between reality and fantasy. As violence is played for laughs and cheers on TV and in the movies, our kids eat their favorite snacks and giggle as the body count rises. We are raising generations of children who learn at a very early age to associate horrific violence with pleasure and excitement—a dangerous association for a civilized society.

This is not to deny the responsibility of parents to "just turn it off," but every single one of the parents of the fifteen shooting victims in Jonesboro could have shielded their families from screen violence and it would not have been enough if the parents of those two little boys didn't turn off their TVs. Let's also understand that as we approach the millennium, we are living in a world where images of violence are literally everywhere, and asking parents to "just turn it off" can help only so much, just as "Just Say No to Drugs," no doubt a worthwhile sentiment, doesn't really tackle that issue's complexities.

A new ingredient in the media violence equation has come with the introduction of violent video games. Screen violence is toxic, whether on TV, in movie theaters, on videotapes, or in video games. But whereas before the children were just "passive" receivers of screen violence, with video games they push the button, click the mouse, and pull the trigger to initiate the carnage and killing. Of course, we all realize that the images on video screens are just that, just as they're not real on TV screens; but the sophistication of this technology is making it hard to tell, especially for children whose minds are not fully formed. And a terrifying new threshold has been crossed with the development of point-and-shoot video games in which the child holds a toy gun and fires away at very real-looking "enemies." What's next? Well, in the coming year we can look forward to Sony's PlayStation 2, which the company claims will challenge our very notions about simulations and clarity of image. After that, who knows how far something like virtual reality will take us.

If you are looking for a direct link between these types of games and increasing rates of violence among children, you need look no further than the events at a Paducah, Kentucky, school a few years ago. Fourteen-year-old Michael Carneal steals a gun from a neighbor's house, brings it to school, and fires eight shots into a student prayer meeting that is breaking up. Prior to stealing the gun, he had never shot a real handgun in his life. The FBI says that the average experienced law enforcement officer, in the average shoot-out, at an average range of seven yards, hits with approximately one bullet in five. So how many hits did Michael Carneal make? He fired eight shots; he got eight hits, on eight different kids. Five of them were head shots, and the other three were upper torso. The result was three dead and one paralyzed for life. I tell law enforcement officers about this when I train them, and they are stunned. Nowhere in the annals of law enforcement or military or criminal history can we find an equivalent achievement. And this from a boy on his first try.

How did Michael Carneal acquire this kind of killing ability? Simple: practice. At the tender age of fourteen he had practiced killing literally thousands of people. His simulators were point-and-shoot video games he played for hundreds of hours in video arcades and in the comfort of his own home. If you don't think these "games" resemble the real thing, you should know that the military and law enforcement communities use video marksmanship training simulators to supplement their training. And the most pervasive simulator the United States Army uses is a minor modification of a popular Super Nintendo game. You should have a look at what's on the market, what's in your home. It is becoming harder and harder to refer to these devices as "games."

The goal of this book is to make people aware of how the prolific use of violence in television, movies, and in video games is affecting our children. We would like to call to the table the makers of this violence so as to address the scientific research on the subject—research that couldn't make clearer the deadly link between this kind of graphic imagery and the escalating incidence of youth violence—and understand and change what they are doing. If by doing this we can prevent future Paducahs, Jonesboros, and Littletons—and these events are really just the tip of the iceberg—I think you'll agree it was worth it.

PAYING ATTENTION TO THE EVIDENCE
BY GLORIA DEGAETANO

I am a media literacy consultant to corporations, school districts, parent groups, and social service agencies. I focus on the effects of television and video on children's development and on solutions to the conditioning effects of media violence. Having spent over twenty-five years in public education, I understand the mechanics of how young brains can be mutated by violent imagery, and, as a parent myself, I speak from the personal challenges of raising healthy children in a society saturated by manufactured horror. My sons are now seventeen and nineteen. I have been a policewoman and a coach throughout their formative years, trying to protect them and often saying no to their desire to play violent video games and watch violent movies and television. Yet at the same time, I encouraged them to think and to question these violent images. I tried to keep their "innocence" as long as possible and, from the very beginning, I wanted them to know in the depths of their beings that they are much smarter and creative than the TV they watch or the video games they play. They can be in control of their visual entertainment. It doesn't have to control them.

In the workshops I conducted for teachers ten years ago, with the research in mind, I predicted that we would soon see more twelve-year-olds committing unspeakable crimes like mass murders. One particular session stands out: seventy teachers listened attentively as I detailed step by step how young brains exposed to a diet of media violence can become conditioned to the actual need for violent entertainment for their "fun." Two other teachers, however, were nonchalantly reading newspapers in the back of the room, thinking themselves invisible. Their ho-hum attitude in the midst of the shocking statistics seemed ludicrous. However, as I began to relay the logical outcomes of such violent input into vulnerable brains, they slowly set their newspapers aside and stared at me. The lightbulb was going on! At the end of the workshop, they told me they knew students who were at risk because of their obsession with violence. Up until then, they hadn't made the link with media violence—it hadn't been laid out before in a way that made sense to them. They were going back to their schools equipped with information to help both the students and the parents.

Misconceptions and misinformation still surround this critical issue. Confusion reigns about what the research says and doesn't say. Talk show debates and rating systems come and go while our children get better and better at killing. How can what's on TV and movie screens and in video arcades make children do such things? After all, we grew up with similar violent images and it didn't turn us into killers. These are valid points—and this issue, like most issues, is not black and white—but the scientific research that links violent imagery on screen with violence among children is out there and has been for many, many years. And no, not every child will, like the two boys in Littleton, walk into their school and start killing people. But all our children are being damaged by heavy exposure to screen violence and in a variety of ways.

The fact is that media violence primes children to see killing as acceptable. Over the years I have heard firsthand many horror stories that show the link between media violence and aggression. Teachers report first graders stabbing kittens to death and mutilating pets after seeing violent acts on TV or in a movie. Parents observe preschoolers attempting to drown siblings because a cartoon hero drowned an enemy on TV. Law officers tell of the hundreds of preteens who plot murder and revenge and luckily are stopped before the tragedy occurs. Adolescents who copy crimes they see on television do so with cold-blooded calculations and without remorse. They even detect and correct the flaws that may have caused the television crime to fail.

It's important to note that media violence can also be a powerful influence for good. Scientific evidence has established that screen portrayals of violence need not lead to reinforcement of aggressive attitudes and behaviors. If the consequences of violence are demonstrated, if violence is shown to be regretted or punished, if the perpetrators are not glamorized, if the act of violence is not seen as justifiable, if in general violence is shown in a negative light as causing human suffering and pain, then the portrayal of violence is less likely to create imitation effects. But if the violence is glamorized, sanitized, and made to seem routine or even fun to do, then the message is that it is acceptable. And our children imitate it. Sensational visual images showing hurting as powerful and domination of others as permissible are dangerous. This is the type of media violence we are challenging in *Stop Teaching Our Kids to Kill.* And we, like President Clinton, are asking the entertainment industry to forgo the massive profits they are generating from this kind of on-screen violence and act responsibly when it comes to our children. Let's face it, we never thought twice about regulating the pornography industry when it involved children, and they never argued that they had a right to target children in their marketing. Why should the standards be different when it comes to something as hurtful and dangerous as violence?

While I know many are very concerned about these issues, I have experienced mothers as being far more outraged than fathers. In fact, over 90 percent of my audiences are female. Many leave my workshops stating, "I wish my husband could have heard this." We certainly need fathers, uncles, and brothers to get more involved in helping both boys and girls see the differences between personal power and domination, between healthy conflict resolution and sick, sadistic forms of expression.

As men and women work together on this issue they can use their unique experiences and perspectives to help each other and to be twice as effective in making necessary changes.

Using this book, parents, educators, social service workers, youth advocates, and anyone interested in the welfare of our children will have a solid foundation for effective action. We give you the facts, the copious, empirical research that exists on the subject, and many ways to make a difference—at home, in your community, and in the larger world—so that we can help end this problem and create a safer environment for us all.

1

IT'S A VIOLENT

WORLD AFTER ALL

IN A FULL-PAGE AD in the June 13, 1999, Sunday *New York Times,* the National Funding Collaborative on Violence Prevention said this: "It should not have taken the Littleton tragedy to focus the nation's attention and energies on preventing violence. . . . It should have been enough that children and adults in our society are victims of violence every day. . . . What is it about violence that we refuse to understand?" Indeed, what does it take to get us as a nation to see that there is a problem? Unfortunately, the increasing number of Littleton-like horror shows is what it takes. Does this make sense? And the problem with our reaction to the Littleton massacre is that we isolate the event; we separate out the actions of Dylan Klebold and Eric Harris from all the violence that is out there, and we in turn lose sight of what the National Funding Collaborative on Violence Prevention refers to as our "culture of violence."

Let's face it, we live in a violent world. We can see it in many aspects of our surroundings, and if we miss it we have a chance to see it played out again and again in the media. There have been countless books and studies on violence in our society and on how to prevent it and what it all means; there will, no doubt, be countless more. But this book is about how that violence, as it is dramatized on-screen in all its various forms, affects our children and conditions them to be more violent than they would naturally become without being exposed to it. Many have reduced this issue to a chicken-and-egg question: does violence on-screen make people violent, or is that violence merely mirroring what is actually taking place every day on our streets and around the world? We think the former, and we have the evidence to prove it. The point is that kids are not naturally violent; they are not born that way, despite what we may think. There are many factors in what makes anyone violent, but the overwhelming proof says that the entertainment industry, through violent programming and video games, is complicit in conditioning our youth to mirror the violence they see on-screen. Much like soldiers, children can and do become learned in this behavior, not by drill sergeants and trained military professionals, but by what they see around them. It seems logical to most of us but is still hotly contested by certain interest groups, and especially in the many levels of the entertainment industry.

But before we present the facts on the negative effects of screen violence on children—how and why it is making them violent—we need to first look at the overall trends of violence at home and abroad—our culture of violence. Essentially, around the world there has been an explosion of violent crime. Experts may disagree on what the statistics mean—many even suggest that all is getting better, not worse—but, in spite of vastly more effective lifesaving technology and techniques, as well as more sophisticated ways of battling crime, the rate at which citizens of the world are attempting to kill one another has increased at alarming rates over the years. According to InterPol, between 1977 and 1993 the per capita "serious assault" rate increased: nearly fivefold in Norway and Greece; approximately fourfold in Australia and New Zealand; it tripled in Sweden; and approximately doubled in Belgium, Denmark, England-Wales, France, Hungary, Netherlands, and Scotland. In Canada, per capita assaults increased almost fivefold between 1964 and 1993. And in Japan, in 1997, the juvenile violent crime rate increased 30 percent.

First and foremost, we must cut through the statistics, which are often easy to misread, and demonstrate just how violent we are and what kind of world our impressionable children are growing up in. Any discussion of the effects that screen violence has on our children must be seen through the lens of our society at large. Also, in order to tackle the seemingly insurmountable problem of violence in our world, we must first see what's actually going on. If we can't be convinced that the rate of violence is increasing, we are not, obviously, going to make a priority of tackling the issue. No problem means no need for a solution.

According to FBI reports, crime is down 7 percent. We are experiencing a slight downturn in murders and aggravated assaults, bringing us back to the crime rates of about 1990. But that is far from the full story. To gain a useful perspective on violent crime—among both youths and adults—the view must cover a long enough time period to clearly identify a trend. Up or down variations over a year or two are meaningless. Until a real trend over a span of years is identified, taking corrective action is difficult and understanding the main reasons for the trend is just about impossible. So what's the big picture of crime in America?

From 1960 through 1991 the U.S. population increased by 40 percent, yet violent crime increased by 500 percent; murders increased by 170 percent, rapes 520 percent, and aggravated assaults 600 percent. In 1996 there were 19,645 murders, 95,769 reported rapes, over 1 million cases of aggravated assault, and 537,050 robberies, amounting to a loss of about $500 million in stolen property.

When applying statistics to the increasing tide of violence, it is important to distinguish between attempts to kill and injure and success at killing. The per capita homicide rate is a measure of how successful we are at killing each other. Murder is the least committed violent crime, although the most often reported crime on the nightly news. Only in the most unusual or extreme circumstances does a case of aggravated assault make the evening news. Yet the rate of aggravated assault clearly demonstrates increasing levels of violence.

We should also note that violent crime statistics are general indicators of the level of violence in society, but not a true measure of the level of violence. The real level of violence will always exceed the level indicated by the crime rates because crimes are not always reported. The level of reporting depends on the type of crime. Virtually all homicides are reported, mainly because as a society we do not allow dead bodies to lie around without investigation. Most robberies of any significant size are reported because someone has lost something of value—and they want to collect on the insurance. But crimes like rape, domestic violence, gang warfare, incidents related to the underworld, and some more minor aggravated assaults (where reporting the incident seems like more of a hassle than it's worth) are underreported. Therefore, we must always take crime statistics with a grain of salt and realize they tell only so much of the story.

However, the crime statistics are really all we have to work with. For the objective side of the story we need these numbers to indicate the changing levels of violence, and these have to be numbers that show changes over reasonably long periods of time. The only available numbers over such periods of time are the above-cited crime statistics from the FBI's Uniform Crime Reports. Figure 1 demonstrates just how bad things have become.

If any one thing sticks out on this graph it is the disparity between the level of murders and that of aggravated assaults. Why, you ask, are they not increasing at the same rate? Consid-

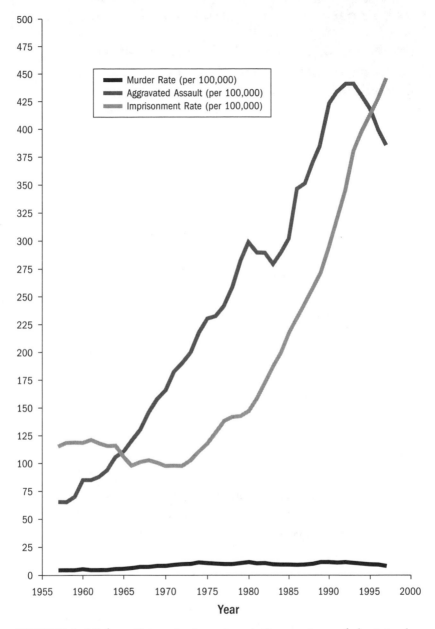

FIGURE 1. Violent Crime in America: A Comparison of the Murder, Assault, and Imprisonment Rates, 1957–1997. (Source data: "Statistical Abstract of the United States." Washington, D.C.: The U.S. Department of Commerce, Bureau of the Census, editions 1957 to 1997.)

ering the advances of our society in the last half-century—major medical discoveries, progressive social initiatives reducing malnutrition and confronting child abuse, a reduction in racial tensions, a booming economy, a sharp reduction in illegal drug use, a quadrupling of the incarceration rate, and advances in law enforcement technology, to name a few, coupled with an aging population—we should have seen a very precipitous decrease in murders and violent crime.

Let's isolate the progress the medical community has made in saving lives. UCLA professor James Q. Wilson is among many experts who have determined that vast progress in medical technology since 1957 (including everything from mouth-to-mouth resuscitation to the national 911 emergency telephone system to advances in medical technology) has helped us save more lives. Otherwise, murder would be going up at about the same rate as attempted murder. Professor Wilson estimated over a decade ago that "if the quality of medical care (especially trauma and emergency care) were the same as it was in 1957, today's murder rate would be three times higher."

This view is corroborated by U.S. Army assessments of wound survivability. According to the U.S. Army Medical Service Corps, a hypothetical wound that nine out of ten times would have killed a soldier in World War II, would have been survived nine out of ten times by U.S. soldiers in Vietnam. This is due to the great leaps in battlefield evacuation and medical care technology between 1940 and 1970. And we have made even greater progress since 1970.

Consider, for instance, some of the advances in medical technology as they relate to treating wounds. Only a century ago, any puncture wound to the abdomen, skull, or lungs created a high probability of death. So did any significant loss of blood (there were no transfusions), most large wounds (no antibiotics or antiseptics), and most wounds requiring significant surgery (no anesthetics, resulting in death from surgery shock).

So, with the medical advances of the last fifty years—not to mention how much better we have become at transporting patients, communicating their conditions, and the speed with which we get them "on the table"—it simply makes sense that the homicide rate would be lower than the aggravated assault rate. We have managed to lessen the rate at which violence is successful in killing people. However, for the past forty years we have not only failed to lessen the rate at which we attempt to kill each other; we have precipitously increased it.

We now know the basic factors that help violence proliferate: poverty, institutional racism, child abuse, and drug abuse. And we are making inroads to understand these problems and do something about them. Of course, it will, in all likelihood, always be argued that we're not doing enough. But think back a few decades. The world was a very different place, some say colder, where child abuse, drug abuse, and racism were for the most part not confronted or dealt with on any significant level. This is not the place to go into how we have come to address the above problems. But societal and technological initiatives abound that are addressing these social factors and that did not exist forty, thirty, or even ten years ago. Shouldn't the advances that have followed these initiatives be contributing to an overall decrease in violence levels? One would think so.

Another way to reduce violent crime is to lock up violent criminals, something that we have been doing at an unprecedented rate. The per capita incarceration rate in America more than quadrupled between 1970, when it was at 97 people per 100,000, and 1997, when it reached 440 per 100,000. According to criminologist John J. DiIulio, "dozens of credible empirical analyses . . . leave no doubt that the increased use of prisons averted millions of serious crimes." Some of those incarcerated are non-violent criminals, but a consistent proportion of them are violent and there can be no doubt that, if not for our tremendous imprisonment rate (the highest of any industrialized nation in the world), the aggravated assault rate and the murder rate would be even higher.

The progress that has been made in law enforcement technology should also be working to keep down violent crime. Excluding well-planned robberies and murders, basic criminal violent behavior has changed little over the last several decades, but the police technology available to apprehend and convict the violent offender has made steady, significant progress. Portable two-way radios, computerized fingerprint systems and ID checks, DNA matching, video monitoring, and many other technological innovations have increased the odds of detection, capture, and conviction, and to that extent should be acting as a deterrent to crime.

Many effective results have also been achieved through ever more innovative and aggressive new police strategies. In Richmond, Virginia, a program of "zero tolerance" for violating federal gun laws (if you are a felon caught carrying a gun you get five years in prison, no exceptions) has been credited with cutting murders by 65 percent. In Boston, Massachusetts, a comprehensive program of nightly home visits by police and probation officers, a zero-tolerance policy for crime and gang activity, and severe punishment for providing guns to gangs and youth led to an 80 percent drop in youth homicides from 1990 to 1995, and in 1996 not a single youth died in a firearm homicide.

We should also see the positive effects of an aging population. The prime years for violent crime are roughly the years from ages sixteen to twenty-four. As the Baby Boomers have aged out of the "prime crime" years the numbers of citizens in their teens and twenties out on the streets has gone down significantly. It might appear that this would help bring down the rate of violent crimes. Yet, throughout this era of an aging population, the violent crime rate still went up.

So the point is made: crime in this country is increasing at an alarming rate and, ironically, most factors suggest it should be doing the opposite. Why, and, most important, where do our children fit into all this?

There are species within ecological systems that are more sensitive than others to environmental stressors. When biologists and ecologists study ecological systems they look at these key species—called indicator species—to understand how severely stressed the systems are. Are our children, socially marginalized and psychologically weakened, the indicator group for the level of violence in our society? Are they the canaries in our coal mines? Unfortunately, the answer is yes. Let's consider some of the statistics regarding youth violence.

- Among young people fifteen to twenty-four years old, murder is the second-leading cause of death. For African-American youths murder is number one.
- Every five minutes a child is arrested in America for committing a violent crime, and gun-related violence takes the life of an American child every three hours.
- A law enforcement survey estimates that there are at least 4,881 gangs in the United States, with about 250,000 members total.
- A child growing up in Washington, D.C., or Chicago is fifteen times more likely to be murdered than a child in Northern Ireland.
- Since 1960 teen suicide has tripled.
- Every day an estimated 270,000 students bring guns to school.
- One of every fifty children has a parent in prison.

Much of this violence is hidden. It doesn't make headlines. Yet many of our children must live with it day in and day out. Consider these facts:

> Bullying: At least 160,000 children miss school every day because they fear an attack or intimidation by other students.
>
> Sexual Abuse: One out of three girls and one out of seven boys are sexually abused by the time they reach the age of eighteen.
>
> Animal Mutilation: Teachers report more and more students as young as seven years old discussing the "thrills" of stabbing a kitten to death or torturing a pet.

As you can see from Figures 2 and 3, youth crime rates, for boys and girls, rose steadily from 1965 to 1985, then took a rather disturbing jump following that. And we hardly need graphs to see it. Children have always been somewhat prone to aggressive behavior, but psychologists are seeing it acted out in increasingly more menacing and deadly ways. In addition, children are becoming more desensitized and complacent toward their own violent acts and those of others. Words and phrases like "rampage," "lockdown," and "body count" have entered into their common language, said in a way that seems harmless enough until you realize what these things really mean. Stephen M. Case, of America Online, says that 80 percent of teenagers on AOL believe that what happened at Columbine could happen in their school. As mentioned above, we obsess on the actions of the kids who take it to the extreme, most likely forgetting that this is just the tip of the iceberg. Dr. Diane Levin, a professor at Wheelock College in Boston, sums it up: "Not only are (our) children hurting each other in ways that young children never did before,

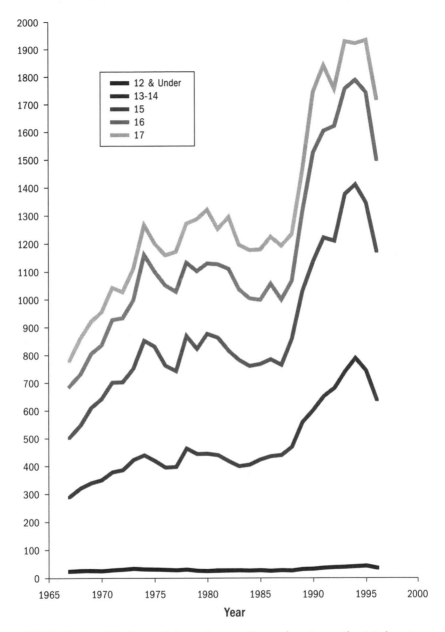

FIGURE 2. Violent Crime Arrest Rate for Juvenile Males (per 100,000). (Source data: Federal Bureau of Investigation, *Crime in the United States 1996, Uniform Crime Reporting Statistics.* U.S. Department of Justice, 1996.)

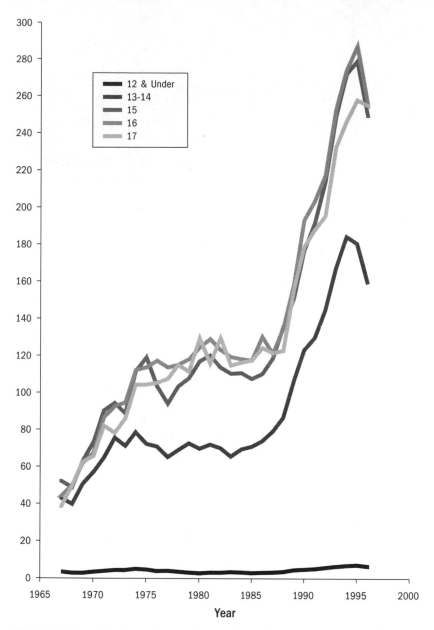

FIGURE 3. Violent Crime Arrest Rate for Juvenile Females (per 100,000). (Source data: Federal Bureau of Investigation, *Crime in the United States 1996, Uniform Crime Reporting Statistics.* U.S. Department of Justice, 1996.)

but they are learning every day that violence is the preferred method of settling disputes."

Think of how benign the term "juvenile delinquent" sounds these days. Kids in the 1950s who were described as such probably got up to some shoplifting, truancy, a fight or two. If they belonged to a gang they might have gotten into a rumble, maybe even a knife fight. But let's face it, you didn't hear about mass killings and terrorist-type behavior when it came to kids. (And it wasn't simply because such things were not reported by the media.) Littleton would have been unfathomable to parents in the 1950s or 1960s, as would metal detectors in schools.

There is something quite disturbing about the kind of violence we are seeing in the schoolyards these days—it's intense. There's a rage out there that wasn't there a few decades ago, and children are settling their differences in scary ways. We weren't shocked to hear that at Columbine High School in Littleton, Colorado, there are preps, jocks, nerds, outsiders—groups of different kids, some popular, some not; some well adjusted, some less so. It's always been that way. Not so great for the kids on the outside, the ones who get picked on and bullied; but they didn't tend to respond to that treatment by killing their classmates and teachers, as Eric Harris and Dylan Klebold did. What has changed enough to cause this? Of course, the world has changed much in the last half-century, but it's hard to identify those factors that would lead to such behavior. Some blame it on increased access to guns. Such access is never a good thing, but we're missing the point if we blame guns; the availability of guns has been a constant factor in the violence equation in the United States. The question we should be asking is why kids want to pick up weapons in the first place. Others blame the decay of societal values. Again, not a good thing for any of us but hardly enough of a reason to explain why children are killing in cold blood. If you run down all the possible factors, the myriad explanations, you will come to rest at one thing: the TV, movies, media, and video games that our kids are spending inordinate amounts of their time with. If you ask what's really changed, that's it—and we all know it. Over the last forty years, slowly, gradually, we have increased the levels of graphic violent imagery on our TVs, in our movies, and at our video arcades. And we have done so under the veil of acceptability. We have put younger and younger children in front of screens depicting horrific violence, and we have done little to address the effects it has had and will continue to have on them. We have no problem letting our children go out and see—or stay at home and watch—"slasher" films, a genre of movie that is aimed at the youth market. We have gone from the benign Pong video game in the 1970s to games in the 1990s that act more as murder simulators and permit youth to mimic the actual experience of killing. And all of this time we have become very good at avoiding the fact that this type of simulated violence has everything to do with the increasing level of violence we have clearly demonstrated in this chapter. Why are we alarmed to find out that the killers in Paducah, Jonesboro, and Littleton were weaned on violent entertainment? And why do we so readily accept the idea that this steady diet of blood and gore had little or even nothing to do with their actions? What do we expect? It's time to hear the evidence.

2

NOT JUST A "TOASTER WITH PICTURES"

Television did have an effect on me right from the beginning. In first grade, I was a member of a four-kid gang that
went around imitating TV westerns. We'd disrupt class to
play out scenes, picking up chairs and hitting people over
the head with them—except, unlike on TV, the chairs
didn't break, the kids did. Finally, the teacher called my parents in and said, "Obviously he's being influenced by these
shows, and if he's to continue in this class, you've got to
agree not to let him watch television anymore." So from
the first to second grade there was a dark period during
which I didn't watch TV at all. And I calmed down and the
gang broke up.

—Brandon Tartikoff, former president of
the National Broadcasting Company

THE DEBATE SHOULD be over by now. Scientific evidence overwhelmingly supports media violence as a major, significant factor contributing to real-life violence in our society—and we'll
prove it. It's a lot to absorb—the findings of key studies in the

last fifty years—but it is of paramount importance that people understand just how much hard evidence exists on the subject. We'll also show you that the entertainment industry has patently ignored the majority of this evidence.

Since 1950 there has been a total of more than 3,500 research studies conducted in America on the effects of media violence on the population. One random analysis of almost 1,000 studies found that all save only 18 (12 of those were funded by the television industry) demonstrate there is a tangible correlation between violent entertainment and violent behavior. So why don't we just stop here and accept that? Would that it were that simple.

One of the problems with convincing people of this relationship is that the proof hasn't been made readily available to the public; many among us do not know the facts and often dismiss the idea out of hand. Also, it is hard, if not impossible, to irrefutably prove a pure correlation. That said, to put it into perspective let us for a moment compare this issue to that of smoking and lung cancer.

There are many contributors to lung cancer besides smoking—the polluted air we breathe, for example—but we have isolated smoking, something we know for certain plays a role in lung cancer, and have made the tobacco industry pay a dear price for selling their product. Studies demonstrate a powerful, statistically significant correlation between media violence and the probability of violent behavior as an adolescent or adult. This kind of correlation data, demonstrating a relationship between two variables (screen violence and violence, or tobacco and cancer) was good enough, by itself, to result in successful legal action against the tobacco industry. But the case against tobacco has always lacked the kind of experimental data with humans that would demonstrate a clear-cut, scientific, cause-and-effect relationship. It is because of this that many scientists have been able to truthfully assert that, in the purest sense, the relationship between tobacco and cancer cannot be proven.

In the realm of cancer research, we cannot inflict cigarettes on every adult and child in one city, region, or nation, while completely denying it to a socially, ethnically, and demographically similar group. But in the realm of media research, the data from this kind of naturally occurring experiment can and has been conducted repeatedly, and always with powerful results demonstrating a clear cause-and-effect relationship between screen violence and violent behavior.

Similarly, it has never been possible to conduct true, controlled, laboratory experiments that expose an experimental group consisting of randomly selected children to cigarette smoke, while also maintaining a similar, randomly selected control group that is not exposed to cigarette smoke, and then demonstrate an immediate, short-term, statistically significant difference between the groups. But in the realm of media violence research scientists over five decades have been able to repeatedly demonstrate both short-term and long-term increases in violent behavior as a result of short-term and long-term exposure to manufactured horror.

We should be clear from the outset: the studies implicate media violence as a major influence; none indict it as the only cause of real-life aggression. Rather, what the studies demonstrate is that violent imagery as a form of amusement for children and youth—who haven't fully developed their thinking functions, who need guidance to analyze and evaluate their experiences, and who have yet to develop accuracy in interpreting and describing feelings spurred by violent imagery—is at very least a dangerous proposition. If adults, with their thinking functions developed, with their abilities to analyze and evaluate intact, and with their language skills proficient enough to express the feelings brought up by horrific images, can still be quite disturbed by violence on-screen, imagine how children and teens are affected and infected. Ours is a media culture careening out of control, with violence everywhere we turn. Understanding the links between real life and screen violence is paramount to taking effective, long-lasting action.

In the myriad studies done over the last four decades, experts have found three basic negative effects from exposure to screen violence: increased aggression, fear, and insensitivity to real-life and screen violence. Some studies highlight one or more of these effects, and other more inclusive, long-term experiments touch on all three.

INCREASING AGGRESSION

Perhaps the most direct effect that screen violence has on children is that it makes them more aggressive, both in behavior and in attitude. As mentioned previously, parents, teachers, and care-givers have noticed an increased intensity in child-on-child aggression. Words turn into pushing faster; pushing turns into punching; and punching turns into further acts of brutality more rapidly than seems natural, or at least than seemed natural a few decades ago. The studies repeatedly demonstrate that we see more physical violence by children and youth who watch screen violence and/or play violent video games. It's that simple. As the content of television becomes more violent, so do our children. Since 1982, television violence has increased 780 percent and in that same time period teachers have reported a nearly 800 percent increase of aggressive acts on the playground. Continual exposure, of course, has more long-lasting effects than short-term episodes.

The possibility that television increases levels of aggression and violence had been raised virtually since the advent of TV viewing in America. The first U.S. Congressional hearings on the question took place in 1952, when only around a quarter of American households had television sets and when what was on TV seemed, by our standards, fairly slow and boring. More often than violence, the "university of the air" brought parents and children programming designed specifically to inspire as well as entertain. Shows like Edward R. Murrow's *See It Now* invigorated adult minds, while children's shows with high educational value flourished. (This is not to say there isn't quality programming today—there most certainly is. Unfortunately, it is being lost in a sea of mindless and violent fare.) By the mid-1950s, however, networks started panicking as they saw where all this quality programming was taking them. American families were turning off their TV sets and talking about what they had just watched. Or some nights they listened to the radio, because for intellectual stimulation it was still a viable medium, and TV's major competition. Neighbors visited each other. The TV was turned off, replaced by conversation and card games. Clearly the networks were not succeeding in gluing families to the tube.

Enter *The Untouchables* and *Gunsmoke*. These violent, action-packed shows immediately captivated adult viewers. Motivated by the urgent need to try something very different, networks stumbled upon the "violence formula." This formula assumes that the more graphic and gratuitous the violence, the more viewers will watch. It works fairly well until levels of violence in real life become comparable to what's on the screen. Then the novelty wears. And the violence levels need to be increased.

In the mid-1950s, as network executives introduced the violence formula, the U.S. Senate began a series of hearings on television violence held before the Senate Subcommittee on Juvenile Delinquency. These procedures began the model of expert testimony on TV violence in front of Congress that is still in place today. During the next few years many highly regarded experts testified that since the risk was so great and the payoff so small, television violence was a totally unacceptable risk. The ball was rolling.

In 1969, Senator John Pastore from Rhode Island, chair of the Senate Subcommittee on Communications, held a hearing to which he invited the usual group of parents, teachers, social scientists, and network executives. He also invited the surgeon general of the United States, something that had never been done before. The surgeon general had just concluded the first report on smoking and health, which caused quite a stir because it indicated a link between smoking and lung cancer. When the surgeon general subsequently commented on TV violence, he put the issue in the same context as the smoking controversy—as a public health issue. This said a lot.

Much of the American public is unaware that many experts have thought of media violence in this context since the late 1960s. The stonewalling of information about the negative effects of media violence has been so great that even today, many physicians, psychologists, and media literacy advocates are under the impression that referring to media violence as a public health concern is a new way to frame the issue. If nothing else, it demonstrates how buried these vital reports have been over the years.

The surgeon general's report, "Television and Growing Up: The Impact of Televised Violence," was released in 1972 and stated that there was strong evidence that TV violence can be harmful to young viewers. Confirming the continually accumulating body of research, this three-year study consisting of sixty new research projects further documented that exposure to screen violence increases the likelihood of aggression.

By 1978, the evidence was piling up. TV violence was making kids meaner and more aggressive. Yet, during this same period, television networks were simply unwilling to keep a consistent stream of nonviolent programming available to the public. They refused to acknowledge the validity of the compelling body of research consisting of hundreds of studies. They would not budge. As network executives manufactured more and more horror for increased profits, they continued to ignore an unquestionable fact: it was our children who were paying the price. And, of course, they knew that. Across the decades the results of studies demonstrating aggression in children and teens after viewing violence on TV or in a movie have held true, whether through measures such as self-reports or through teachers' observations. And they continue to hold true for more recent studies in which the measures of aggressiveness have become more sophisticated.

In 1982, the National Institute of Mental Health issued a pivotal report. This was a review of over 2,500 studies on the effects of TV violence—about fourteen volumes of documentation. The conclusion indicated a consensus among members of the research community that ". . . in magnitude, television violence is as strongly correlated with aggressive behavior as any other behavioral variable that has been measured."

The year 1984 brought the findings of a very significant twenty-two-year longitudinal study by Professors Leonard Eron and L. Rowell Huesmann. These pioneering researchers followed the fates of 875 children living in a semi-rural U.S. county. Taking into account their baseline aggressiveness, intelligence, and socioeconomic conditions, it was found that, for both boys and girls, the amount of television they were watching at age eight predicted the seriousness of criminal acts for which they were convicted by age thirty. This was a big, and frightening, leap to make. It pushed the evidence one major step forward.

Perhaps scariest of all is the fact that Eron and Huesmann further observed second-generation effects: Girls and boys watching more television at age eight were later, as mothers and fathers, punishing their own children more severely than those parents who had watched less television as children. Remarkably, how much television violence a thirty-year-old parent had been watching at age eight predicted their children's degree of physical aggressiveness even better than it predicted their own at age thirty! It is something to consider that these second- and now third-generation effects are accumulating and rippling down through the generations during today's era of unprecedented youth violence.

The mid-1980s brought another seminal study, this time by Tannis McBeth Williams. Her 1986 conclusions were reminiscent of what you have just read about on the screen violence/aggression equation; but what is fascinating is how she conducted her experiment. She and her associates at the University of British Columbia investigated the effect of the introduction of television upon the children in a remote, rural community, called Notel, for "No Television."

Researchers studied both children and adults before television was introduced into Notel and two years after its introduction, and compared these results to those from two other communities that had television. The children and adults in Notel showed a significant increase in physical and verbal aggression after the two years. Also, children as well as adults more often used aggressive behavior as a successful and acceptable method for achieving goals.

With the introduction of television, young children's behavior changed more significantly than that of older children or adults. Forty-five first and second graders in the three towns were observed during free play for rates of objectively measured noxious physical aggression—such as hitting, shoving, and biting—before television was introduced into Notel. The same forty-five children were then observed again during free play two years later. To prevent bias in the data, the research assistants collecting the data were actually kept uninformed as to why they were observing children in these three towns for rates of hitting, shoving, and like behavior. Furthermore, an entirely new set of research assistants was employed the second time around, so that a data gatherer would not be influenced by some recollection of the child's behavior two years earlier.

As would be expected, rates of noxious physical aggression did not change in the two control communities, since they had already been exposed to television to begin with. In contrast, by two years after the introduction of television, rates of physical aggression among Notel's young children had increased by 160 percent! The increase was observed in both boys and girls, in those who were aggressive to begin with and in those who were not.

Even though social scientists had been studying the relationship between television and aggression for several decades, what is perhaps the most telling indictment did not come from social scientists, and it did not start as a study of television. By 1981, the rate of real-life violence had risen to the level where it was *finally* being identified as a public health issue. Dr. Brandon Centerwall, M.D., an epidemiologist, was asked to help start the violence research program at the National Centers for Disease Control in Atlanta, Georgia. A central issue confronting the research team was the doubling of the murder rate in the United States since the 1950s. That the rate had doubled was indisputable. The question was, why?

Dr. Centerwall approached this as a question of epidemiology, searching through rigorous statistical analysis for the causes of the "epidemic of violence." He considered every possibility that any research evidence had ever suggested might reasonably be a cause, including changes in urbanization and economic conditions; the effect of the post–World War II baby boom; trends in alcohol abuse, capital punishment, and civil unrest; changes in the availability of firearms; and television. Television was included as part of the array. It was not considered more likely to provide an explanation than any of the other proposed candidates.

Over seven years of research, first at the Centers for Disease Control and later at the University of Washington, Dr. Centerwall gathered statistical data and tested the various factors to see if a causal relationship with the rising level of violence could be identified. One by one, as the research evolved, factors were eliminated for significant causal relationships. Yet each time the television hypothesis was subjected to the testing, it quite stubbornly refused to be eliminated. As each of the other candidates dropped away, television slowly moved to front and center.

After testing rigorously for confounding cross-relationships with other possible causes, the conclusion was inescapable. And the process of arriving at the epidemiological conclusion was so gradual that, in Dr. Centerwall's words, "There never was a moment of 'Aha!' It simply happened."

After painstaking testing all over the world, Dr. Centerwall blew the roof off the subject by stating that if "television technology had never been developed, there would today be 10,000 fewer murders each year in the United States, 70,000 fewer rapes, and 700,000 fewer injurious assaults."

As mentioned, there have been thousands of like studies that have come up with similar conclusions. Centerwall's study sticks out for his method—and for the jaw-dropping nature of his indictment of television violence. The results of this study were published in a "special bulletin" in the *Journal of the American Medical Association* in 1992. If the study had told us that 10,000 people per year were dying from an infectious disease, it would have made the evening headline news. Alas, almost nobody in this country has heard of Dr. Centerwall or his findings.

DESENSITIZING US

Another effect of screen violence on children—and, for that matter, adults—is that they become more desensitized to violence and less outraged by its effects. Callousness toward brutality sets in and a "so what?" attitude begins to frame the context by which horrific acts are seen. Consequently, more justification for violence takes place in the minds of these individuals. Images of violence as "cool" serve to reinforce deviant attitudes and result in less empathy, compassion, and understanding for human suffering.

Violence does not occur solely via an attacker's aggressiveness. Violence is also caused by the unwillingness of others to intercede. To update Edmund Burke, it is sufficient for violence to flourish that bystanders do nothing. In a classic 1974 study, fifth-grade children were randomly assigned to watch either fifteen minutes of a television crime drama—including several shootings and other violent acts—or fifteen minutes of a televised baseball game. Afterward, the investigator left each child in charge of supervising the behavior of two younger children by means of a television monitor. "I imagine they'll be okay," they were told. "But sometimes little kids can get into trouble, and that's why an older person should be watching them. If anything does happen, come get me."

After the investigator left, the television monitor showed the two younger children getting into a quarrel, which then escalated into threats and physical blows; finally, the camera was knocked over and, amid shouts and crashing, the monitor went dead. (Unbeknownst to the older children, the fight was taped, not live, so all children witnessed exactly the same sequence.) As compared to the children who had watched the baseball game, the children who had just finished watching fifteen minutes of television violence were five times more likely to simply fail to summon help.

Cultural insensitivity is also demonstrated by our increased ability to tolerate more and more graphic displays of violence in the media. Hyperviolent movies such as *Natural Born Killers,*

Pulp Fiction, or *The Matrix* would not have been tolerated, let alone achieved commercial success, in 1939—the year that *Wuthering Heights, The Wizard of Oz,* and *Gone With the Wind* were released. PG-rated *Dick Tracy,* one of the more benign movies of the 1990s, with only fourteen slayings, had a higher body count than the original 1974 *Death Wish,* which by many people's standards was a really violent film. The definition of what is socially acceptable, even normal, alters according to our level of desensitization. "Simple" violence becomes passé; seeing a few dead bodies makes little or no impression on us. Body counts rise, violence is more graphic, real. And we soon start feeling comfortable with the kind of ultraviolence now seen regularly on television and at the movies. Another way we become desensitized to such violence is when it's presented without some kind of redeeming message. In 1990, social critic Mark Crispin Miller said this: "In *Bullitt* (1968) and *The French Connection* (1971), in *The Searchers* (1956), and in movies of Sam Peckinpah, the violence, however graphic, was muted by a deep ambivalence that shadowed even the most righteous-seeming acts of vengeance, and that therefore suppressed the viewer's urge to join in kicking. In contrast, screen violence now is used primarily to invite the viewer to enjoy the feel of killing, beating, mutilating." The point being, viewing violence for its own sake is a destructive trend. Our children get nothing out of it except the message that violence is okay, even fun.

We can also measure our cultural insensitivity by what we deem appropriate viewing for children. For instance, the Power Rangers show, popular with toddlers and preschoolers, contains about two hundred acts of violence per hour. It's interesting to note that the adolescents who are now committing horrendous crimes in Jonesboro, Paducah, and Littleton, were weaned on *G.I. Joe* and *She-Ra*—cartoons averaging twenty-five acts of violence per hour. In contrast, adult shows contain far fewer acts of violence per hour.

Perhaps our cultural desensitivity about age-appropriate fare can be best understood in comparison to other countries. It was common for American preschoolers to see the Batman movies or, especially, the Teenage Mutant Ninja Turtle movies, during the 1990s. Most parents didn't think twice about it. However, it's interesting to note that British children under the age of twelve were not allowed to see Batman, and Swedish children under the age of fifteen could not get in to see the first two Turtles movies.

This increase in the level of violence on-screen, and the accompanying increase in desensitivity that it inflicts on children especially, means that the entertainment industry must up the ante (twenty-five acts of violence per hour to two hundred!) to hold and, certainly, to increase viewership. The more often our children are exposed to violent programming, the more it is seen as normal and natural—and the less attention-grabbing it becomes. If screen violence seems like an addictive drug, you're on the right track. The more one takes in, the stronger the next dose must be in order to attain the same level of response. The fact that all forms of media violence, whether on TV or in film and video games, have become more and more graphically brutal and sensational attests to the effectiveness of desensitization.

INCREASING FEAR

The third symptom of violence as entertainment is increased fear in our society. A constant diet of violent portrayals can make people more distrusting and exaggerate the threats of violence that really do exist. Nightmares and long episodes of anxious behavior are common for young children exposed to violence on TV or in a film.

Violent and/or scary TV programs and movies have both immediate and long-term effects on children. Immediate reactions include intense fear, crying, clinging behaviors, and stomachaches. Long-term reactions vary from nightmares and difficulty sleeping, concern about being hurt or killed, and aversion to common animals. In her book, *Mommy, I'm Scared: How TV and Movies Frighten Children and What We Can Do to Protect Them,* Joanne Cantor, Ph.D., asks: "How much fright can a child take? When does the spine tingling cease to be fun? . . . There have been several case studies in medical journals telling about young people who had to be hospitalized for several days or weeks after watching horror movies such as *The Exorcist* and *Invasion of the Body Snatchers.* One recent article reported that two children had suffered from post-traumatic stress disorder, a diagnosis usually reserved for Vietnam War veterans and victims of physical violence, as a result of watching a horror movie on television. One of the children described in the article was hospitalized for eight weeks."

By watching violence, both children and adults can come to see the world as a much more dangerous place than it really is, and act upon those misperceptions. Research on trauma suggests that all it takes is one terrifying experience, especially for children, to form a lifelong memory, one that it is difficult to erase. Some 23 million Americans suffer from some sort of anxiety-based disorder. Is exaggerated, irrational fear some part of the modern condition? Stephen Hall, in an article in the *New York Times Magazine,* points out: "It may be one of the paradoxes of our age that we've created entire economies around activating this fear system under safe conditions in the form of theme-park rides and Stephen King novels and films that have us on the edge of our seats."

Most of us protect our children from the violence that exists on the street, mainly because we don't want them to be physical victims of it but also because we are painfully aware of how exposure to it will skew their world perception. So what sense does it make for us to allow them to be saturated with images that frighten and terrorize?

George Gerbner, a distinguished researcher currently at Temple University, has been studying the content of TV violence in prime time and in children's cartoons and the effects of that content on both children and adults for over twenty years. In 1990, he and Nancy Signorielli released a significant body of work that showed that a steady diet of violent programming caused both children and adults to see the world and other people as more dangerous than they actually are. He called this effect "the mean world syndrome."

Gerbner and his associates have tracked public perceptions of society in relation to the respondents' extent of television viewing. Those who watch five or more hours of television daily are more fearful than those who watch three hours or less. Heavy viewers are more apt to overestimate the chance that they will be victims of crime (greater than FBI crime reports for their locale would suggest). These people have also taken more precautions than others, such as limiting their travel at night and changing the security in their homes. They look out for themselves more, trust others less, and see the world quite differently than do those who do not perceive the possibility of violence at every turn.

The research demonstrated that TV violence distorts a person's concept of reality, changing his or her attitudes and values. Thus, TV creates a perceived need for guns, which in turn creates violence, which reinforces the "need" for guns, and so on, in an endless, tragic spiral.

As our children were becoming more aggressive, desensitized, and fearful, TV violence continued to escalate. A 1994 study by the Center for Media and Public Affairs identified 1,846 violent scenes on network and cable programs between 6 A.M. and midnight on one day in Washington, D.C. Most of these were of an extremely horrific nature, and without context or judgment about social acceptability. The most violent periods were between 6 and 9 A.M., with 497 violent scenes, or 165.7 per hour, and between 2 and 5 P.M., with 609 violent scenes, or 203 per hour. These are the times of day when children and youth are most likely to be watching. This is no coincidence. The study also concluded that from 1992 to 1994 depictions of serious violence increased 67 percent, violence in promos and trailers almost doubled, and violence in network and local news programs increased 244 percent.

We must remember that this fallout in the early 1990s was the result of years of "all talk and no show" on the part of the networks. Remember Newton Minow's "vast wasteland" speech of 1961? Minow, then the newly appointed chairman of the FCC, sat down and watched one full week of television in preparation for his inaugural address to the National Association of Broadcasters (NAB). Minow's advice to the broadcasters of the 1960s could be addressed to them today (except that today our "stations" never go off the air!):

> I invite you to sit down in front of your television set when your station goes on the air and stay there . . . until the station signs off. I can assure you that you will observe a vast wasteland. You will see a procession of game shows, violence, audience participation shows, formula comedies about totally unbelievable families, blood and thunder, mayhem, violence, sadism, murder, western bad men, western good men, private eyes, gangsters, more violence and cartoons.

Although broadcasters responded to Minow's speech by agreeing to assign large parts of the UHF spectrum to public broadcasting, they did not take violent programming off the air, nor reduce violent content. The "vast wasteland" remained a metaphor for television content throughout the 1970s.

In 1981, the newly appointed chair of the FCC, Mark Fowler, prepared for his inaugural address to the NAB in the same way Minow had—by watching a week of television. However, Fowler came to the opposite conclusion. Instead of a vast wasteland, he saw a "vast richness," despite the fact that TV violence had increased significantly since 1961.

Fowler said that television was just another appliance, "a toaster with pictures," and that we need not be concerned. Yet, in the 1980–81 season, when the FCC was discussing deregulation of children's programming, violence on children's television shows reached its highest level in twenty years: thirty-three acts of violence per hour. The deregulation came in 1984, and with it more reason for concern. Now, for the first time, toy manufacturers could develop thirty-minute cartoon "commercials" for their products. The sponsors, companies from the toy industry, basically began to overrun the television industry. By 1987, the sales of violent toys had soared more than 600 percent. Cartoons, more violent than ever, flooded the market, along with their icon toy counterparts with which youngsters could practice violent play while they weren't watching. Action figures based on popular cartoon characters acted as enablers to our children's TV violence addiction.

Then all the commotion began. Congressional hearings in the late 1980s resulted in the Television Violence Act (TVA) of 1990. This legislation provided the television industry with temporary antitrust immunity so that they could work together to develop "voluntary guidelines" on television violence.

Also in 1990, the Senate and the House passed the Children's Television Act, but President Bush refused to sign it, saying it bordered on infringement of the First Amendment. He did, however, allow it to become law. The Children's Television Act made two provisions:

1. Commercials during children's programs could not exceed 10.5 minutes per hour on weekends and 12 minutes per hour on weekdays.
2. Television broadcast licenses could not be renewed unless the station had complied with the first provision and had served the "educational and information needs of children" by providing at least three hours a week of educational programming.

In the coming years, many experts and parents would decry the lists of programs that networks identified as "educational." The networks deemed such programs as *G.I. Joe, Leave It to Beaver, The Jetsons,* and *James Bond, Jr.* as examples of shows that served the educational and informational needs of children.

Clearly the industry regarded the Television Violence Act and the Children's Television Act as a joke. And we found that, tragically, the joke was on us. The 1990 report, "Watching America," which had reviewed six hundred prime-time television shows, analyzed TV's portrayal of the society it is supposed to serve. Its conclusions were certainly not a laughing matter:

> Our studies show that an evening of prime time puts to shame a night at the [police] station house. Violent crime is far more pervasive on television than in real life, and the disparity widens as the danger increases. For the most serious crime of all, the difference is most dramatic. Since 1955 television characters have been murdered at a rate of 1,000 times higher than real-world victims.

Yet, two years later the networks were still in mass denial. The words of Barry Diller, at the time chairman of Fox, Inc., typify the extent of this denial: "The issue [of TV violence and its effects] is so complex, it's not appropriate to deal with this in some superficial way. . . . I don't think we know enough yet." How much more could he possibly want to know?

By 1992, the industry, having been forced to do so by the TVA, had established a set of guidelines. Within this venue, at this time, before this audience, they simply could not deny the many negative effects of TV violence any longer, and thus found themselves to be morally and legally obligated to construct what they called a "Statement of Principles." Note that, while Congress had demanded the establishment of a set of "guidelines," what the industry created were "principles." Being forced to establish guidelines (or principles) by no means forces the industry to follow them. Consider some of the following text and compare it to what you see on your television today. If you see a wide disparity, you're not alone.

- Children's programs should attempt to contribute to the sound, balanced development of children and to help them achieve a sense of the world at large;
- Violence, physical or psychological, should be portrayed only in a responsible manner and should not be used exploitatively. Where consistent with the creative intent, programs involving violence should present the consequences of violence to its victims and perpetrators;
- Presentation of the details of violence should avoid the excessive, the gratuitous, and the instructional;
- The use of violence for its own sake and the detailed dwelling upon brutality or physical agony, by sight or by sound, should be avoided;

- Particular care should be exercised where children are involved in the depiction of violent behavior.

The fact that the television industry came up with such principles strongly suggests they knew what they should be doing—what was right. But it doesn't take much research at this point to figure out that they ignored their own advice. And sure enough, more pressure from Congress and the threat of restrictive legislation prompted the cable industry to sponsor the three-year (1996–1998) National Television Violence Study (NTVS) at a cost of $3.5 million. (The broadcast industry, not to be outdone, also financed its own three-year study during this time period at a cost of $1.3 million.)

The National Cable Television Association (NCTA) awarded a three-year contract to Mediascope, Inc., to administer the largest study of television content ever undertaken. Mediascope, in association with the Universities of California, North Carolina, and Texas, was selected to conduct the research after a competitive process that attracted proposals from many leading experts in media research.

In February 1996, the first-year analysis was released. It is important to note that this study was the most comprehensive evaluation of its kind. Unlike past studies, this project did not merely count the number of violent acts and report them. Rather, the researchers developed nine contextual features to measure the harmful effects of that violence. For instance, they determined that television violence poses the greatest risk if there are repeated acts using a conventional weapon, if violence is put into a humorous context, or if it is morally justified in some way.

The conclusion of the first year of the study was that "psychologically harmful" violence is pervasive on broadcast and cable TV programs. The NTVS found not only that 57 percent of programs contained some violence, but also that the context in which this violence occurs can have harmful effects.

In 1997, the second-year summary of the research was released, with similar results. And in April 1998, third-year results told the same story and made a mockery of the networks' "principles" and the so-called cooperation on the topic of reducing TV violence. Facts such as these emerged:

- Nearly 40 percent of the violent incidents on television are initiated by characters who possess qualities that make them attractive role models.
- One-third of violent programs feature "bad" characters who are never punished.
- More than half of the violent incidents feature physical aggression that would be lethal or incapacitating if it were to occur in real life.
- At least 40 percent of the violent scenes on television include humor.
- 60 percent (up 3 percent from the 1996 results) of television programs contain violence and more than 60 percent of the violent incidents involve repeated behavioral acts of aggression.
- Youngsters who watch two hours of cartoons each day are exposed to five hundred high-risk portrayals of violence per year that teach aggressive behaviors.
- TV ratings tend to attract many children to very violent, inappropriate programs by alerting kids to their existence.

Marty Franks, senior vice president of CBS, strongly disputed the study. He said his network's prime-time lineup featured programs with little violence. Franks claimed: "This study persists in using the same flawed methodology that led several years ago to the twenty-fifth anniversary of *Laugh-In* being named that year's most violent program by simply counting acts of violence without taking dramatic context into account."

False.

As stated above, the National Television Violence Study was the most comprehensive television violence study ever, incorporating extensive contextual features. The bottom line is that the networks have reverted to gross misrepresentations of the vast body of research in this area.

In response to the National Television Violence Study, the American television industry simply rewrote their own history by perpetuating a quarter-century of smoke screens and denials. In fact, television violence continued to escalate both on cable and noncable networks over the three-year period of the study. What the industry did to try to divert attention from the core of the problem was to inaugurate both the rating system and the V-chip (a device that parents can use at home to block violent programming).

Writing about the fallout from the industry-supported research, Dr. George Comstock, Newhouse Professor at the S. I. Newhouse School of Public Communication at Syracuse University, pointed out: "What had begun as a concern over the harmfulness of violent portrayals, and especially in regard to the facilitation of antisocial behavior on the part of viewers, became an endeavor simply to inform parents so that they could better govern their children's viewing. . . . The social and behavioral sciences have empirically identified a problem and offered a solution (however difficult): the reduction of harmful portrayals. If the problem is those . . . harmful effects, then labeling content for the V-chip exorcism will succeed only if all households comply. And if they were to do so, then there would be no need for the V-chip because the incentives to produce such content would be absent. The industry has substituted appearance for substance."

While U.S. network executives and film producers continued with wide-eyed innocence to plead ignorance of the vast amount of evidence, the rest of the world was penning their indictment for the perpetuation of the new "global aggressive culture" that was being marketed to children.

In 1998, the seminal work "Children and Media Violence: A Yearbook from the International Clearinghouse on Children and Violence on the Screen" was released by UNESCO. This is a four-hundred-page book describing worldwide studies of media violence, including the largest study ever conducted, which surveyed five thousand twelve-year-olds in twenty-three countries, and it thoroughly and irrevocably supported what studies for the last four decades have been literally screaming at the world and the entertainment industry. How much clearer can it possibly get?

We may have as a society been fascinated by violent imagery over the decades. But things are changing—at least for adults. After five decades of escalating media violence, the public is showing signs of having had enough. A recent study examining 2,380 major movie releases from 1988 to 1997 indicates that the film industry produced 17.4 times more R-rated than G-rated films, yet G-rated films produced 8.35 times more profits per film than R-rated movies. PG-rated movies were second in profits, followed by R-rated, then NC-17 movies.

If the film industry is profit-driven, what drives the making of the R-rated violent films? If the TV industry has spent millions of dollars on their own studies demonstrating the validity of the scientific research, why do they continue to increase violence levels? Why is it that the broadcast industry is not following the very guidelines they themselves established? How can there even be any more argument when everyone in the industry agrees that thirty-second television commercials change adult behavior? If rapidly moving images and inane jingles flashed on a small two-dimensional screen can get adults to do things, why would violent images watched for hours on screens large and small have no impact on the behaviors of children and teens?

Along with the science has come the advice from the experts in child development. Yet the industry has refused to listen both to the evidence and to the purveyors of that evidence. Pediatricians, psychologists, educators, and experts on youth violence have taken on the enormous responsibility of making the industry pay attention and make significant changes. The responsibility should be reversed. It is not up to the child-care experts to get the industry to listen. They have no leverage to do that. We need to realize that when it comes to our children's viewing habits, the *real* media critics are not Roger Ebert and other journalists but rather the AMA, the APA, and the American Academy of Pediatrics. If the TV and movie industries truly had the interest of America's children in mind, they would actively engage the broad, mainstream consensus—not just hire a few "experts" who basically agree with them. The entertainment industry has taken the approach of "How much poison can we put in the food and get away with it?"

As a result of all this undeniable research, many experts and organizations with moral and social responsibility for children's welfare have issued strong statements over the years. When organizations representing all of America's doctors, all of her psychiatrists, and millions of parents, call upon an industry to change (i.e., reduce violence on the public airwaves), and then that industry does exactly the opposite (i.e., increases the violence), this can be viewed as nothing short of complete and total contempt for the people of the United States.

The evidence is in. The debate is over. And we can no longer wait for the TV executives and movie moguls to change. As you will see in the next two chapters, the stakes are too high, way too high, for that.

3

PRETENDING

TO BE

FREDDY KRUEGER

MANY BELIEVE THAT the desire for murderous violence is largely unnatural. For example, it is rare for animals of the same species to fight to the death. In their territorial and mating battles, animals with horns will butt their heads to establish domination. They do not kill each other with their potentially lethal horns. However, against any other species, they turn their heads to the side with the intention to gut and gore. Similarly, piranhas will fight one another with raps of their tails, but they will turn their teeth on anything and everything else. Rattlesnakes wrestle each other, but they do not hesitate to turn their fangs on another species. It is suggested that this tendency is innately imprinted into the genetic code in order to safeguard the survival of the species.

Although primates, both in the wild and in captivity, have been known to murder one another, apes, gorillas, and chimpanzees do not have near the assault or murder rates we humans do. What we have witnessed in animal behavior indicates that such acts of violence by primates are usually the result of a lot of provocation combined with complex social anomalies. And they are rare. Only humans have come to kill each other easily.

One major modern revelation in the field of military psychology is the observation that this resistance to killing one's species is also a key factor in human combat. Brigadier General S. L. A. Marshall first observed this during his work as the chief historian of the European theater of operations in World War II. Based on his innovative technique of postcombat interviews, Marshall found that only 15 to 20 percent of the individual riflemen in World War II fired their weapons at an exposed enemy soldier.

Marshall's findings have been somewhat controversial, but every available, parallel scholarly study has validated his basic premise. Paddy Griffith's data on the extraordinarily low killing rate among Napoleonic and American Civil War regiments, Richard Holmes's assessment of Argentine firing rates in the Falklands war, the FBI's studies of nonfiring rates among law enforcement officers in the 1950s and 1960s, and many other individual and anecdotal observations all confirm that humans, by nature, are not close-range, interpersonal killers.

Violent behavior is nurtured over time. We attest that, due to overexposure to gratuitous violent imagery, our children undergo a systematic conditioning process that alters their cognitive, emotional, and social development in such ways as to embed in them a desire and/or conditioned reflex to act out violently without remorse. In this chapter we will discuss the first part of this process, which argues that children's long-term exposure to violent television and movies makes them easy bait for the conditioning effects of violent video games, the next stage of the process. When both processes are followed rigorously, we may have killers on our hands. And we do.

THE ENVIRONMENT TEACHES

Conditioning our children and teens to want and need to act out violently starts with environmental saturation of visual violence. John Dewey, the great education innovator, once said, "The environment teaches." What he meant by that simple statement is that what surrounds the child also teaches the child. Even if you cannot remember a second of your own childhood, have no children of your own, or have never, for some reason, witnessed the actions of a child, you should know that children learn from what's around them. It's an inalienable truth. So consider the following:

- A preschooler who watches about two hours of cartoons a day is exposed to nearly ten thousand violent episodes each year. At least five hundred of them feature a potent set of contextual features, making them a high risk for teaching aggressive attitudes and behaviors.
- Nearly 40 percent of all the violent incidents on television are initiated by characters who possess qualities that make them attractive role models to kids. More than half of these incidents feature physical aggression that would be lethal or incapacitating if it were to occur in real life.
- By age eighteen, a typical American child will have seen at least 200,000 dramatized acts of violence and forty thousand screen murders.

When it comes to the question of what our children are learning, the answer is simple: violence, mayhem, and murder. Dr. Alvin Poussaint, professor of psychiatry at Harvard Medical School, has stated that exposing children to violent media images is "abuse" similar in effect to physical or sexual abuse or living in a war zone. "None of us," says Dr. Poussaint, "would willingly put a child into those situations, yet we do not act to keep them from watching movies about things we would be horrified to have them see off the screen." Why is this so? Why, as a society, do we not see the link between violence on-screen and violence off-screen? Have we become too good at coming up with excuses? "I grew up with violent movies and television, and I don't want to go out and kill somebody." Or, "The images are not real, and my kid understands that. It's just harmless fun, like playing with toy soldiers." Thinking this way is an easy way out, but it is just not realistic. And, again, we do not dispute that there are many children out there who can absorb screen violence ad infinitum and grow up to be normal, happy, healthy, nonviolent adults. But there are many more who cannot, and for all kinds of reasons.

Excuses like the ones above are misguided. As a society, we have never before had to deal with the huge quantity or intensity of violent imagery as we do today. We have never before on such a massive scale sat toddlers in front of harrowing brutality. In the last thirty years a relatively modest number of channels has turned into a television universe of more than ninety channels, all of them easily accessible. Nor have so many children and teens used vicarious deviancy as real-life amusement as they do today. So we can't compare our own experiences growing up to our children's. It's not accurate, nor is it fair. As home and community environments saturate children with images of sensational violence, a gradual process of systematic desensitization and conditioning begins—not unlike what recruits are put through in the military. They're broken down, desensitized with constant abuse, endless physical repetitions, and their existing mores and norms are replaced with a new set of values that embrace destruction, violence, and death as a way of life. The difference is that the military has two safeguards: the process of turning someone into a soldier includes powerful doses of discipline and character development; and they're doing it to adults. It may seem like a stretch to most, but this analogy holds true on the many levels in which screen violence affects the young.

Marines start their training at eighteen; children start a lot earlier than that. From a very early age, a taste for visually vivid depictions of human death and brutality is slowly nurtured in our kids. In American culture, toddlers as young as eighteen months begin with TV programs especially designed for them that contain twice as much violence as adult prime-time viewing. By preschool age, the child is inundated with tangible reinforcers of screen violence that many parents think are necessary for the child's appropriate acceptance into the peer group. These include action-figure toys, clothing, coloring books, lunch boxes, and other merchandise promoting the latest popular, violent TV programs, movies, or video games.

Since the Mouseketeers hawked Mickey's ears and Davy Crockett made a furry cap the rage with young wanna-bes, merchandising to children has been an integral part of media entertainment. What has changed drastically since then is the type of violent play our youngsters conceive and act out. And it is due, in large part, to screen influence and the proliferation of the accessories that basically provide a "rubber stamp" for increasingly more deviant forms of "child's" play.

Aggressive play is a normal part of a young child's experimentation. In fact, parents who refuse to buy toy guns for their youngsters report that guns will be made out of sticks, carrots, toilet rolls—basically anything children can get their hands on. This is a normal process. So, too, it is normal for children to imitate what they see on the screen in their play. What is not normal, however, is the almost exclusive acting out of violent roles over and over, so that the media-induced violent images become the sole source for the child's play fantasies.

In today's world, youngsters' play is no longer inner-directed and originally created. In the past, TV characters or movie heroes were a part of a generative play experience. The children incorporated the media images into original ideas such as the re-enacting of the trip to the grocery store taken earlier or the anticipated vacation to the beach. Screen characters would be within a context that included a broad range of characters from children's real-life activities. The child might be an action figure one day, a postal worker another day, a gardener, bus driver, a mom, dad, teacher, film star. Remember when we were worried that children were playing doctor and nurse? Children would imitate a broad range of adult roles. No longer.

The restrictive aspect of young children's play is currently a major concern of early childhood educators around the nation. Child-care providers often see that the child who veers from the narrow script of a violent TV program is ostracized by his or her peers when playing. Children who pretend to be teachers rather than Power Rangers are just considered "weird."

Writing in *Psychology Today* in 1975, the renowned cognitive psychologist Jerome Bruner stated: "It [children's play] is the vehicle of improvisation and combination, the first carrier of rule systems through which a world of cultural restraint replaces the operation of childish impulse." In 1975 children were imitating social rules and norms in their creative play more often than they were imitating deviant visual images. So as they acted out their play scenarios, socially acceptable behaviors were being reinforced as youngsters learned to communicate with each other, express feelings, negotiate differences, resolve conflicts. What social "rules" are being reinforced as children act out TV programs that model and reward physical aggressiveness? How can youngsters possibly learn "social restraint" if their creative play consistently models the impulsive violent behavior they see on the screen?

The most popular children's television shows in 1995 included *Spider-Man, Mighty Morphin Power Rangers, Masked Rider,* and *X-Men.* All of these programs contained extremely violent behaviors perpetrated by fantasy heroes. Also, each of these programs produced an entire line of toys and other licensed products. Visual messages of domination, revenge, and physical abuse become easier for our youngsters to act out when they are surrounded by merchandise reinforcing those messages. The World Wrestling Federation sells action figures "with bone-crunching action" to children ages five and up.

By the teen years, how do we then take back the cumulative impact of applauding violent behavior as a normal problem-solving technique, natural tendency, and acceptable social norm? "No, we didn't really mean for you to take us seriously. It's all just in fun. No one takes those wrestlers seriously. You must know Bruce Willis didn't mean it's okay to hurt someone else. Do you think killing your teacher will solve your problem? You can't be serious, can you?"

FIRST IMITATION, THEN IDENTIFICATION

The impact of violent imagery on children is best understood within the context of normal child development. Children are born with an instinctive capacity and desire to imitate adult behaviors. That infants can, and do, imitate an array of adult facial expressions has been demonstrated in newborns as young as a few hours old—before they are even old enough to know that they themselves have facial features that correspond with those they are observing and imitating. Babies as young as fourteen months old clearly observe and incorporate behaviors seen on television.

Emotionally laden images are even more efficient at catching and holding the attention of youngsters than educational demonstrations. Because kids attend so readily to the visually exciting and emotional portion of the screen content, this violent imagery is so much more easily remembered and learned by children under eight or nine years old. They respond to emotional content with feelings such as fear and fright, but they are unable to put graphic visual images and the emotions they arouse within an understandable framework. Also, young children are unlikely to pick up on the subtlety of the images' mitigating information—such as negative motivations, punishment that occurs later in the program, or the suffering of victims—and put it into some kind of context.

For example, there is the case of a preschooler who expressed fear and hostility toward black people after watching *Roots* on television with her family. After describing a vivid scene in which a slave gets repeatedly whipped, the child said that the man being whipped must be a very bad person, and therefore must be very scary.

Young children have an instinctive desire to imitate the behavior of others, but they do not possess an instinct for gauging whether a behavior ought to be imitated. They will imitate anything, including behaviors most adults would regard as destructive and antisocial. Since youngsters do not have the brain capacity yet for analysis, evaluation, or moral judgment, they are developmentally unable to discern the difference between fantasy and reality; if they did, we wouldn't have too many kids believing in Santa Claus or the Tooth Fairy. Therefore, they are incapable of interpreting violent images, of making personal sense out of them.

The inherent inability to distinguish fantasy from reality, although developmentally appropriate, means that, in the minds of young children, media violence is a source of entirely factual information regarding how the world works. Studies indicate that "real" to a young child appears to mean physically existing in the world. They may regard police dramas to be real because police officers do exist. One second-grade student in a study explained that the members of the Brady Bunch were real because "they have a refrigerator, and there are such things as refrigerators."

And there is no limit to a child's credulity. For example, an Indiana school board had to issue an advisory that stated that there is no such thing as Teenage Mutant Ninja Turtles—that they do not exist. Too many children had been crawling down storm drains looking for them.

When a young child sees somebody being shot, stabbed, raped, brutalized, degraded, or murdered on TV, to them it is as though it is actually happening. Imagine children of three, four, or five watching "splatter" movies in which they spend sixty minutes learning to relate to a cast of characters and then in the last sixty minutes of the movie they watch helplessly as their newfound friends are hunted down and brutally murdered. This is the moral and psychological equivalent of introducing a child to a group of new friends, letting them play with those friends, and then butchering them in front the child. And this happens to many children again and again throughout their early development.

While children experience cognitive confusion about what they see on the screen, that does not keep them from imitating violent behaviors. In fact, the more often children watch violent television programs and movies, the more likely it is that they will develop and sustain highly aggressive heroic fantasies for years to come. Then, in a vicious cycle, the children who create violent fantasy play and who identify with aggressive heroes are the ones most likely to be affected by media violence.

Here's a scary scenario: A seven-year-old boy described a deliberate attempt to reduce his own fear by identifying with a character in *A Nightmare on Elm Street*. "It was easy," he said. "I pretended I was Freddy Krueger. Then I wasn't scared. Now, that's what I always do and I am never scared." Since identifying with an aggressive hero can increase real-life aggression, this tactic for reducing fear is chilling indeed.

Learning is carried out in two stages: imitation and identification. At the beginning, learning comes through imitation; with enough repetition, identification takes place. As kids imitate the violence they see on-screen through imitative play, they are learning to identify themselves as perpetrators of violence . . . from the very beginning of their lives! It has been found that the more unrealistic the character, the more preschoolers both want to be like that character and think they are like that character. Also, young children are more likely to choose fantasy heroes over real-life heroes in their play, more likely to engage in more heroic adventure play, and more likely to learn about heroes and play themes from television rather than from friends, siblings, or parents.

Children with a propensity for violence usually have both learning and behavior problems and are labeled "difficult" by teachers and parents. From the onset of their formal schooling years they come to identify themselves as bullies and schoolyard thugs. They not only use violence as a mainstay of amusement and imitate it at every opportunity, but also identify themselves as violent people. Early childhood is a formative time of ego development. We all know an adult who doesn't believe us, no matter how much we tell them they are pretty, smart, and capable. They see themselves as ugly, stupid, inept. They see themselves that way largely due to the messages they received about themselves as children. Recurring childhood messages impress young minds. Once believed, they are very difficult to change later in life.

Everything the young child experiences and learns is latent, ready for the right circumstance to trigger future behaviors. Serious violence is most likely to erupt at moments of severe stress—and it is precisely at such moments that adolescents and adults are most likely to revert to their earliest, most visceral remembrance of violence. Consider the power of such violent "imprinting" on a little boy who watches his dad beat his mom repeatedly. He is two, three, four, or five years old and he despises this behavior and he hates his father. But if he is not careful, twenty years later, when he is under stress and he has a wife and kids, what is he likely to do? He will do the same thing he saw his father do. Why? He, of all people, should understand how despicable this behavior is, how much his children will hate him. How much he'll hate himself. But he can't help it—it was burned into his system at an early age and imprinted on how he deals with like situations.

Now consider that this little boy not only observes domestic violence, but is also physically abused himself. He distracts himself from the pain he experiences by watching television. Like 56 percent of children between twelve and seventeen in our country, he grows into later childhood and early adolescence by escaping to his bedroom and watching TV or rented videos. He likes watching violence. The violent imagery, in fact, reinforces and justifies the violence he is experiencing in the home. How much more likely is it that he will become a violent abuser himself?

An estimated four million American children are victimized each year by physical abuse, sexual abuse, domestic violence, community violence, and other traumatic events. When television is added to this equation, more stress is added to the child's life. Research has found that abused children watch more television than other children do, prefer violent programs, and appear to admire violent heroes. Children who are both abused and watchers of a great deal of television are most likely to commit violent crimes later in life.

However, many of the twenty million children in this country are experiencing a form of abuse in the constant bombardment of violent visual messages throughout their childhood and adolescence. All are being imprinted with visual directives that make violence socially acceptable and that encourage violent self-expression. The severity of that imprinting is dependent upon the degree of violence in the child's home environment, the amount of screen violence taken in daily, and the beliefs the child holds about his or her self and the world.

UPSETTING YOUNG BRAINS

The brains of violent people are different from the brains of non-violent people. Violent or aggressive people have decreased activity in the prefrontal cortex, leading to troubled thinking and problems in the left temporal lobe, leading to a short fuse. How do adult brains come to have such problems? There are a number of reasons, but could saturation with violent, fast-paced screen images play a significant role?

The brain of the child is not a miniature version of the adult brain. Although the child's heart is a miniature replica of an adult heart and the lungs tiny versions of future adult lungs, the young brain is an organ that will change considerably as it matures over the course of childhood and adolescence. As it builds neural structures for optimal development, the young brain is very vulnerable to stimulus from its environment. A lack of the proper kinds of stimulus, combined with the wrong kind of stimulus at inappropriate times, can cause permanent damage.

In today's world the proper kinds of stimulation needed for children to develop healthy brains are being displaced by so much time spent in front of a screen. Children growing up as spectators, staring at two-dimensional images for four or more hours daily, do not get enough physical movement, tactile, 3-D experiences, problem-solving practice, or opportunities for language expression and skill-building that they would get with less time watching and more time doing. These real-world activities are absolutely vital. Without them, the cortex, including the vital prefrontal cortex, which acts as a dampening switch to impulsive behavior in healthy and mature adults, cannot develop appropriately.

In addition to displacing activities imperative to healthy brain development, a fixation with violent on-screen images can alter the brain's alert system, causing more hyperactivity and impulsive behaviors. Violent images keep the story plot or the video game moving fast and the excitement high. The low brain, the seat of our survival instinct, stays ever on alert. When this part of the brain is preoccupied with danger, the cerebral cortex, or seat of rational thought, is hard-pressed to function optimally.

Screen violence can increase the reactivity of the brain stem. Children's hearts race, their eyes bug out, their breathing comes in gasps as they munch on snacks and watch the body count soar. The brain's alarm network, known as the "fight or flight mechanism," sits at the base of the brain and sends out noradrenaline pathways to other brain centers that control heart rate, breathing, blood pressure, emotions, and motivation. As the highly charged screen images constantly assault the brain, the noradrenaline gauge rises, keeping the body in a constant state of readiness—easy to startle, quick to blow up. In effect, violent images keep the instincts and feelings keenly aroused while reducing thinking functions.

Television and movie violence overstimulate our children and overstress their brains. The faster and the more salient the violent imagery, the more likely it is that our kids will be in states of emotional arousal. It is the fast action and the quick cuts of today's programming that keep the young brain on alert, in a way very similarly to the soldier who is on alert in the battlefield, or an abused child who is on alert for the next slap.

Children of abusive parents tell how they huddle together with their siblings and listen, with their hearts racing, to their tormentor's steps on the stairs, the jingle of his keys, the sound of his voice. When the abuser is in view they watch him constantly, never taking their eyes off of him. Like feral animals, they have learned at an early age the habit of vigilantly monitoring their environment for any sign of danger.

This capacity to identify and monitor sources of potential violence and danger in our environment is a powerful survival mechanism. But when children are in constant threat of danger, they become hypervigilant. They continue to monitor their environment for perceived threats even when they are in a safe environment.

While violent images are keeping our kids on alert, they just sit there. There is no way to release the energy building up inside them. Unless the child can discuss the feelings associated with those horrific images with a caring adult, those feelings have nowhere to go. Feeling scared that Freddy's going to get you when you go to bed? Feeling like it might be cool to carry a gun, as your hero does? Feeling fascinated with all the blood and gore, yet slightly ashamed about that at the same time? Feeling sexually aroused at the beating of a near-naked woman and very guilty at the same time? How do our kids understand and disperse all the feelings that watching violence arouses? Unfortunately, most children and teens don't get these vital opportunities. There's no one around to talk with them at these crucial moments. As a society, we have deemed TV and videos our number one baby-sitter. It gives us a needed break, to hop in the shower, get dinner on the table, or just read the newspaper and unwind after a busy day. But if we don't know what that baby-sitter is spitting out at our kids, we are all, children, parents, and society, paying a huge price.

Instead of learning to put the emotional reactions within a thoughtful context, instead of struggling to make sense out of the sensational and find some way to understand what is happening, kids cheer, boo, whistle, yell, and continue to promote a hyped feeling state. The thinking function has taken a vacation.

Hearts can become desensitized when minds stop making connections. Where does a conscience come from? Our lower brain with its survival mechanism, quick to react to any perceived threat, can't help us here. It's the developed mind with a well-equipped imagination that gives us the capacity for compassion. When we say to a child, "Imagine what it's like to be homeless," the first prerequisite is that the child must have an imagination. In order to have any inkling of empathy for the homeless, the child must have a thinking function for understanding and an imaginative ability for visualization. And those capacities cannot and will not develop as our children consume violent images, alone, for fun.

How often do we now hear of kids being indifferent to the violent crimes they commit? In Florida, for instance, a six-year-old boy and his friend got into a fight in his apartment. Finally, to end the matter, the boy maneuvered his friend out onto the balcony and pushed him over the railing, sending him to his death ten floors below. Twenty minutes later, the police came upstairs to ask some questions. The boy was watching cartoons on television. During the questioning, the boy continued to watch cartoons and eat pizza. He was perfectly calm.

How can a child become this desensitized? When children start off in an alarm state with high noradrenaline and impulsive behavior, they often revert to low noradrenaline levels and calculating behaviors. Brains in a constant hyped state get worn out and sociopathic behaviors are the result. You need only recall when Michael Carneal, the fourteen-year-old boy who killed three classmates in Paducah, Kentucky, or Andrew Golden, the eleven-year-old killer in Jonesboro, Arkansas, were brought to court to face their crimes. Their eyes looked dead, they betrayed nothing physically or emotionally that would suggest they had just gunned down children in cold blood. We want to see some remorse; instead we see nothing that would indicate that these young boys understood their actions.

Research indicates that children may be deliberately trying to conquer their fears of vulnerability and victimization by desensitizing themselves through repeated exposure to horror movies.

But to the extent that they desensitize themselves to screen violence and fear, they are also becoming more tolerant of violence in the real world. And more tolerant of themselves as perpetrators of violence.

Dr. William Belson interviewed 1,565 youths who were representative of thirteen- to seventeen-year-old boys living in London. These boys were interviewed on several occasions concerning the extent of their exposure to a selection of violent TV programs broadcast over a twelve-year period. The level and type of violence in these programs was rated by the BBC viewing panel. It was thus possible to obtain, for each boy, a measure of both the magnitude and type of exposure to televised violence. Also, each boy's behavior was determined by a self-report indicating involvement in any of fifty-three categories of violence over the previous months. The degree of seriousness of the acts reported by the boys ranged from taunting to more serious and violent behavior. The boys reported atrocities: "I forced a girl to have sexual intercourse with me; I bashed a boy's head against a wall; I threatened to kill my father; [and] I burned a boy on the chest with a cigarette while my mates held him down." After controlling for one hundred other factors, it was found that boys who had watched above-average amounts of television violence were currently engaged in rates of serious violence 49 percent higher than that of boys who had watched below-average quantities of violence.

Constant exposure to screen violence can profoundly affect both children and adults in two important ways: we can come to need a daily dose of violent media, and we can build an immunity to violent imagery, becoming incapable of producing socially acceptable emotional responses. As our kids desire increased levels of violence and become more and more desensitized, they are constantly learning that harming is fun, "natural," and the "right" thing to do.

To make humans continue doing something naturally repulsive, you make it fun for them. This is called classical conditioning. The Japanese army very effectively used classical conditioning with their soldiers. Early in World War II, Chinese prisoners were placed on their knees in a ditch with their hands bound behind them. And one by one, young, unbloodied Japanese soldiers had to go into the ditch and bayonet "their" prisoners to death. This is a brutal, horrific way to have to kill another human being. Up on the banks, their friends would cheer them on in their initiation to violence. Afterward, they were treated to the best meal they'd had in months, sake, and "comfort girls." The result? They were not just desensitized to violence; they were taught to enjoy violence, to associate human death and suffering with pleasure.

This technique is so morally reprehensible that there are very few examples of it in modern U.S. military training. Yet every day children of all ages and in all stages of brain and ego development watch vivid pictures of human suffering and death for fun and come to associate horror with their favorite soft drink, candy, girlfriend's perfume, birthday party celebrations, or comfort in the hospital bed.

Once the brain solidifies the link between pleasure and violence, it is difficult to convince it that it isn't normal to do so. Endorphins remember. The thrill of seeing violence becomes "cool," the rush repeatable. Columbine was horrifying. What about all the youths who reportedly wanted to imitate the violence after Columbine? How horrifying is that?

Every state had their share of such children—children who thought the events at Columbine were overwhelmingly "cool." Children who talked about repeating the tragedy—not from the victims' perspective, but from the murderers' viewpoint. The emotional reaction for the normal teen ought to be outrage, anger, revulsion, and disgust toward the perpetrators and empathy and compassion for the victims. And, don't get us wrong, we do realize that many kids have these feelings. But too many do not, and not long ago such attitudes would have been clearly defined as sick and twisted. We have to be careful. The increasing number of "normal" youths expressing the abnormal desire to kill other human beings may be desensitizing us. Are we forgetting what is normal behavior for our children? Are we lowering our expectations and standards as our children change?

AIDS doesn't cause people to die. Rather, it destroys the immune system and makes the victim vulnerable to death by other factors. The "violence immune system" exists in the human brain. The conditioning of our children by violent visual entertainment creates an "acquired deficiency" in this immune system. AVIDS, "Acquired Violence Immune Deficiency Syndrome," weakens appropriate cognitive, emotional, and social development, causing more children to become increasingly vulnerable to other violence-enabling factors in our society such as poverty, discrimination, drugs, and the availability of guns. Children with weakened violence immune systems also become increasingly vulnerable to conditioning. Their attitudes, behavior, and values change as a result.

Although only a small percentage are currently committing violent crimes, many of our kids are developing AVIDS. We are losing the battle as parents to condition our children to be responsible, caring, peaceful, intelligent individuals. And it should not be happening. When you think about it, we shouldn't have to contend with such overt negative influences. There are enough real-world negative influences bombarding children as it is. Sure, our children just might come out of their younger years unscathed, well-adjusted, and nonviolent—but it's getting harder and harder for them to do so.

4

"IT'S IMPORTANT TO FEEL SOMETHING WHEN YOU KILL"

LIKE MOST TECHNOLOGIES, video game technology has changed drastically in the last few years. Arcades may look much the same on the surface as they did a decade or two ago, but the games have become far more violent, sophisticated, and addictive. Pac-Man they are not. In case you haven't made a trip to a video arcade lately, or peered over your child's shoulder while he's standing in front of the television pointing and shooting something that looks suspiciously like a real weapon, then you should. If Pong—or, for that matter, Pac-Man and Super Mario Brothers—is your point of reference, think again. We must assume that what we know of the more benign, outdated games of the 1970s and 1980s, even of the early 1990s, and the research regarding them, cannot be considered valid for the games that have been put on the market in the last five years. It's a whole new world, and it's evolving at a rate that is hard for parents to keep pace with.

How fast a rate? Consider this: During the last two decades interactive video games have emerged as one of the most popular forms of entertainment, particularly among teens. According to the nonprofit organization Mediascope, "Globally, annual video game revenues now exceed $18 billion. In the United States alone, video game revenues exceed $10 billion annually, nearly double the amount Americans spend going to the movies. On average, American children who have home video game systems play with them about ninety minutes a day."

The kids are changing with the technology—how could they not be? They are riding the technology curve in a way we are not and never can. On many levels it's wonderful to have them exposed to this brave new cyberworld; the opportunities for them to learn, the resources at their fingertips, are tremendous and hard to fathom. The World Wide Web is like a vast, almost limitless encyclopedia, and unlike *Encyclopaedia Britannica*, kids can talk to it and it talks back. So it's especially disconcerting to see armies of these very kids wandering through cyberspace mutilating and killing everything in their path—and having a great time doing it. It's the dark side of heightened technology, but one to which we ought to be paying much closer attention.

More than any other aspect of these new video games, it's the accuracy of the simulations—the carnage, the blood, the guts—that is so advanced. Realism is the Holy Grail of the video game industry. And the latest technology leaves little to the imagination—the simulations seem less fake, and therefore more effective. Compare it, if you will, to a well-made horror movie with a very believable plot, set in a town not unlike your own, with characters that could be right out of your neighborhood. The reality of it will undoubtedly affect you, more so certainly than watching a low-budget picture like *Godzilla*.

So, immersed as we are in technology in all facets of our lives, it's not hard to understand why children's games are more advanced and sophisticated—they're like everything else these days. But the fact that, in the last few years, video game manufacturers have chosen to amplify gruesome violence (note that 49 percent of young teens indicate a preference for violent games, while only 2 percent prefer educational ones), to make it a mainstay in their products, seems a direct result of where the television and movie industry have taken *their* content.

The relationship between viewing violent television and films and being attracted to these elevated forms of interactive violent video games is well documented. We've talked a lot about the desensitizing effect on-screen violence has on kids, and how it fosters a need for more graphic, real-life displays of carnage and mayhem to keep kids interested. The entertainment industry knows this better than anyone, and the makers of these games are way past the curve. Graphically violent video games like Doom, Postal, Duke Nukem, and Mortal Kombat serve up just what the doctor did not order.

And you can see why. The real selling point with these games is that you get to pull the trigger, you inflict the damage, rather than just watching someone else do it. As graphic as the violence is on TV and in movies, it can't quite compete with a medium where you, not an actor, can control the action. It's a whole new level of involvement—and it's terrifying.

Any teacher or coach of young people will tell you that hands-on experience is what teaches best. Repetition of movements and the hand-eye connection are invaluable for learning most skills. And, especially with children, hands-on learning is usually a lot more fun and interesting than the alternatives. It's precisely this that makes interactive video games so potent a learning tool. As researcher Patricia Greenfield points out, "Video games are the first medium to combine visual dynamism with an active participatory role for the child." Television, film, and video game violence may all be imaginary, but the latter lets you put your hands on it, aim, and fire. We don't think we have to tell you how deadly the combination can be of viewing ultraviolent images with the amusement park fun of shooting at things until they drop.

So it's no surprise that violent video games are very habit-forming. Parents we have spoken to are alarmed at not just the violent images in the games but the amount of time their children spend playing them. If nothing else, it proves how effective these things are. More than 60 percent of children report that they play video games longer than they intend to play. The interactive quality, the intensity of the violence, the physiological reactions, all serve to connect the player's feelings of exhilaration and accomplishment directly to the violent images. And "good" feelings keep the player wanting to play. Countless parents try desperately to keep video game play within certain time limits, but it's a huge challenge . . . a parental battle we often lose. Once kids get hooked, it's difficult to unhook them. Both home and arcade games make extensive use of reinforcement schedules for both the acquisition and maintenance of the habit. According to Jane Healey, in her classic book *Endangered Minds,* here are the basic elements that make video games addictive:

1. The player experiences feelings of mastery and control. The less sense of power the child or teen feels in his or her life, the more this element may become important as an addictive factor. (In fact, studies show that generally boys' preferences for violent video games are associated with low self-competence—in school, in personal relationships, and in general behavior. For girls, more time playing video or computer games is associated with lower self-esteem.)

2. The level of play is exactly calibrated to the player's ability level. Rather than coping with the challenging problems in the real world, young people are easily drawn into following the more made-to-order sequence in video games.

3. The player receives immediate and continual reinforcement, which make the games particularly addictive.

4. The player can escape life and be immersed in a constructed reality that seems to be totally in his/her control. (We all know that one of the anxieties of being young is a lack of control. Parents, teachers, clergy, and caregivers tell you what to do, and it's not always very much fun. It's one reason why children have active imaginations and like to construct their own worlds. And it's usually healthy for them to do so—if they are exercising their own imagination. Video game manufacturers understand this desire—and they give kids all the things they want, and for as long as they're willing to stick with it.)

As children and youth are playing these games for ten or more hours a week, they are not solving and negotiating conflicts with their peers, and they are missing priceless opportunities to gain needed cooperative learning and social skills. Instead, the world constructed for them by video game manufacturers comes to determine their ability levels for successful negotiation with people in the real world. The more they become inept at dealing effectively with real-world people and situations, the more likely it is that they will lose themselves in the video games, particularly violent ones that ensure feelings of control, mastery, and exhilaration. And as the real world of slowness and struggle, decisions and demands becomes less appealing, children's psychological and physiological systems become more affected by violent video games.

In a study on arcade use among adolescents, "regular" arcade visitors varied from the more "casual" visitors (those who visited less often) in their orientation to, and experience in, arcades. Regular visitors were more likely to score positively on indices screening for addiction. This study raised important questions about children's vulnerabilities to potentially addictive technologies and their access to violent video games at arcades.

But children do not have to go to arcades to become addicted to video games. Home video games can have the same effect. "A definite drug response" is how Dr. Donald Shifrin, a pediatrician and the American Academy of Pediatrics representative on the National Television Violence Study, describes what he sees when children and teens play video games at home. "When youngsters get into video games the object is excitement. The child then builds a tolerance for that level of excitement. Now the child mimics drug-seeking behavior . . . initially there's experimentation, behavior to seek the drug FOR INCREASING LEVELS OF EXCITEMENT, and then there is habituation, when more and more of the drug is ACTUALLY NECESSARY for these feelings of excitement. There is no need to have a video game system in the house, especially for young children. There is no middle ground for me on this. I view it as a black-and-white issue like helmets for bike safety. If parents want, rent a video game for a day and then return it. Everyone goes to Disneyland for a day. No one goes there DAILY."

Are children and teens who regularly play violent video games in a permanent state of arousal? We know that merely watching violent imagery physiologically arouses both children and adults. Early experiments using physiological measures of arousal such as galvanic skin response, heart rate, and respiratory changes found that children are emotionally responsive to even animated television violence. If being a spectator to the sensational arouses our children, what happens when they get to engage in the simulated slaughter?

The effects of violent video games on young adults' arousal levels, hostile feelings, and aggressive thoughts have been measured. Results indicated that college students who had played a violent virtual reality game had a higher heart rate, reported more dizziness and nausea, and exhibited more aggressive thoughts in a posttest than those who had played a nonviolent game.

Another study examined differences in cardiovascular reactions and hostility following nonviolent play and violent video game play. The subjects were thirty male college undergraduate students. Only male subjects were used because most video games are male oriented, males frequent video game arcades more often than do females, and the gender gap in video game play widens with age until the undergraduate years. Hostility and cardiovascular reactivity were examined after subjects played either a nonviolent game of billiards or a violent video game. The video game, Mortal Kombat, was presented in either a less violent (MK1) or a more violent (MK2) version. Results indicated that subjects who played the video game had higher heart rate reactivity than those who played billiards. Subjects who played the MK2 version showed greater systolic blood pressure reactivity than those who played the MK1 version or billiards. Subjects who played MK2 scored higher on the hostility measures than those who played MK1, who in turn scored higher than those who played billiards.

These two studies indicate that adults, with fully developed brains and central nervous systems, can be impacted negatively by violent video games. What about children and teens whose brains and response mechanisms are in the process of development? They are much more vulnerable to physiological arousal and conditioning effects.

A real—and the newest—concern we have with our children's exposure to violent video games is what the devices teach them physically. The mechanical, interactive quality of a "First Person Shooter" game like Doom or 007 Golden Eye makes it so much more dangerous to society than images on a television screen, however violent. "Why?" we are constantly asked. "It's a game. It may be violent and it's probably better our children weren't exposed to it, but . . ." Well, it's a lot more than that. Certain types of these "games" are actually killing simulators, and they teach our kids to kill, much the same way the astronauts on Apollo 11 learned how to fly to the moon without ever leaving the ground. Believe it or not, simulators can be that good. Sounds far-fetched, we know. But consider the following.

The military learned in World War II that there is a vast gulf, a leap, between being an ordinary citizen and being someone who can aim and fire a gun at another human being with intent to kill, even in war. They discovered that firing at bull's-eye targets in training did not properly prepare soldiers for combat. Bull's-eye targets are not humans; they are not even simulated humans. And shooting at a bull's-eye target may teach someone the mechanics of aiming a gun, pulling the trigger, and dealing with the recoil, but it doesn't teach what it takes to look at another human being in the eyes, lift up a weapon, and knowingly try to take their life. Soldiers in that war spent a lot of time firing their guns into the air or not at all. In fact, the firing rate was a mere 15 percent among riflemen, which, from a military perspective, is like a 15 percent literacy rate among librarians.

The army's first simulators used "simulated people" or silhouettes as targets, and that appears to have been sufficient to increase the firing manyfold. But pop-up targets, firing ranges, and bullets are expensive (bullets for a 9 mm pistol cost over twenty cents each). Improved technology now allows these communities to train on computer simulators—to learn how to shoot, where to shoot, how to maneuver through possibly deadly combat situations, how to tell enemy from friend, and, most important, how to kill. The entire event of killing in combat can be simulated by a computer.

There are three things you need in order to shoot and kill effectively and efficiently. From a soldier in Vietnam to an eleven-year-old in Jonesboro, anyone who does not have all three will essentially fail in any endeavor to kill. First, you need a gun.

Next you need the skill to hit a target with that gun. And finally you need the will to use that gun. The gun, the skill, and the will. Of these three factors, the military knows that the killing simulators take care of two out of three by nurturing both the skill and the will to kill a fellow human being.

Operant conditioning is a very powerful procedure of stimulus-response training, which gives a person the skill to act under stressful conditions. A benign example is the use of flight simulators to train pilots. An airline pilot in training sits in front of a flight simulator for endless, mind-numbing hours; he is taught to react in a certain way when a particular stimulus warning light goes on. When another warning light goes on, a different reaction is necessary. Stimulus-response, stimulus-response, stimulus-response. One day the pilot is actually flying a jumbo jet, the plane is going down, and three hundred people are screaming behind him. He's scared out of his wits, but he does the right thing. Why? Because he's been conditioned to respond in a particular way to this crisis situation. He reacts from a conditioned response rather than making a cerebral decision. Thinking too much in these types of situations may mean that you will be dead before you do something effective.

Today soldiers learn to fire at realistic, man-shaped silhouettes that pop up in their field of vision. This "simulated" human being is the conditioning stimulus. The trainee has only a split second to engage the target. The conditioned response is to shoot the target, and then it drops. Stimulus-response, stimulus-response, stimulus-response—soldiers and police officers experience hundreds of repetitions of this. Later, when they're out on the battlefield or walking a beat and somebody pops up with a gun, reflexively they will shoot, and shoot to kill.

These devices are used extensively, and the scientific data on their effectiveness is exhaustive. It began with flight simulators and tank crew simulators half a century ago. Their introduction is undeniably responsible for increasing the firing rate from 15 to 20 percent in World War II to 95 percent in Vietnam. In the Falklands war, the Argentine soldiers, trained to fire at bull's-eye targets, had a firing rate of approximately 10 to 15 percent. The British, trained to kill using modern methods, had well over a 90 percent firing rate. Thus we know that, all other factors being equal, 75 percent to 80 percent of the killing on the modern battlefield is a direct result of the simulators.

Now these simulators are in our homes and arcades—in the form of violent video games! If you don't believe us, you should know that one of the most effective and widely used simulators developed by the United States Army in recent years, MACS (Multipurpose Arcade Combat Simulator), is nothing more than a modified Super Nintendo game (in fact, it closely resembles the popular game Duck Hunt, except with a plastic M16 firing at typical military targets on a TV screen). It is an excellent, ubiquitous military marksmanship–training device. The FATS trainer (Fire Arms Training Simulator), used by most law enforcement agencies in this country, is more or less identical to the ultraviolent video arcade game Time Crisis. Both teach the user (or player) to hit a target, both help rehearse the act of killing, and both come complete with guns that have recoil—the slide slams back when the trigger is pulled.

In a bold advertising campaign, the brochure for the home version of this game, in particular, asserts: "Time Crisis uses the revolutionary Guncon, the most advanced light gun ever made for any home system. The Guncon connects to the video output of the PlayStation and it actually stores the screen image in the gun button so players can duck and reload. . . . It's time we got the handguns off the streets and back where they belong—in the hands of America's youth."

We're not the only ones suggesting that violent video games and military simulators share the same technology. The wording in this ad for the game device WingMan Force puts it as bluntly as is possible: "[WingMan Force is] based on the same exacting technology used for aerospace, medical and military stimulators. It uses high-precision steel cable drives so you can actually feel the detailed environment of your favorite games . . ." The ad goes on to remind us, "Psychiatrists say it is important to feel something when you kill."

The military and law enforcement agencies across the country are none too pleased that these devices are in the hands of civilians, especially kids. In a lawsuit against the video game manufacturers that has come out of the killings in Paducah, Kentucky, the heads of several major national and international law enforcement training organizations have offered to testify that these video games are identical to law enforcement firearms training devices, except with the safety catch turned off. That should say a lot. The video game industry boasts about the real quality of their products; the military and police are wondering why on earth such technology is on the street. What more proof do we need that these games are anything *but* games?

Across America we are reaping the bitter harvest of this "training" as ever more kids shoot their girlfriends or their teachers or other individuals that they have grudges against. A horrific development in this is that rather than just stopping with their intended target, these kids keep firing—and a simple grudge turns into a mass murder. The point is, these games are indeed affecting our children and we can't hide behind the myriad other excuses when kids "go off." Because when they do, they do so in all the ways these games train them—to kill every living person in front of them until they run out of bullets or run out of targets. That results in a lot of dead bodies.

Michael Carneal, the fourteen-year-old boy who walked into a Paducah school and opened fire on a prayer group meeting that was breaking up, never moved his feet during his rampage. He never fired far to the right or left, never far up or down. He simply fired once at everything that popped up on his "screen." It is not natural to fire once at each target. The normal, almost universal, response is to fire at a target until it drops and then move on to the next target. This is the defensive reaction that will save our lives, the human instinctual reaction—eliminate the threat quickly. Not to shoot once and then go on to another target before the first threat has been eliminated. But most video games teach you to fire at each target only once, hitting as many targets as you can as fast as you can in order to rack up a high score. And many video games give bonus effects . . . for head shots. It's awful to note that of Michael Carneal's eight shots he had eight hits, all head and upper torso, three dead and one paralyzed. And this from a kid who, prior to stealing that gun, had never shot a real handgun in his life!

In South Carolina a boy named Wesley Schafer had put hundreds of dollars into point-and-shoot video games. One day he and a buddy of his decided it would be fun to rob the local convenience store. They walked in and Schafer pointed a .38 caliber pistol at the clerk's head. The clerk turned to look at him, and the defendant shot reflexively from a range of about six feet. The bullet hit the clerk right between the eyes and killed him. Afterward, police asked the boy what had happened and why he'd done it. Killing the clerk clearly was not part of their plan—it was being videotaped from six different directions. Schafer responded, with great anguish and confusion, "I don't know; it was a mistake; it wasn't supposed to happen." Stimulus-response.

In the Jonesboro, Arkansas, shootings, one of the two children (eleven and thirteen) involved had a fair bit of experience shooting real guns, but the other boy, to the best of our knowledge, had none. These two avid video game players fired a combined total of twenty-seven shots from a range of over one hundred yards, and hit fifteen people. They strategically trapped their victims, lined them up, and shot with deadly accuracy. Battle-scarred veterans and military analysts reacted with amazement at the accuracy of their shooting, on one hand, and the military strategy involved in setting up their "kill zone," on the other. Both skills are taught by an array of home and arcade video games.

The incident that really brought the issue to the public's attention, though, was the Columbine High School massacre, in Littleton, Colorado. It was well documented that Dylan Klebold and Eric Harris were literally obsessed with playing the video game Doom and other such games. And they were very good at it. These boys, like the other boys mentioned, practiced for hundreds and hundreds of hours, perfecting their craft. Therefore, it should not be altogether surprising that their killing spree resembled something out of the cyberworld of a typical Doom scenario. (In fact, Eric Harris reprogrammed his edition of Doom so that it looked like his neighborhood, complete with the houses of the people he hated.) They moved from room to room, stalking their prey and killing almost everyone in their path. And, not unlike most kids' response to video game mayhem, Dylan Klebold and Eric Harris laughed the killings off.

The realism of a game like Doom, played on the home computer, can be extreme, especially with the multitude of "add-on" packages available to upgrade systems. For example, in the wake of the Columbine massacre, many in the game industry claimed that Doom, played only with a mouse or keyboard, can't possibly teach a player real combat skills. First, we have to understand that even when Doom is played with a mouse, it is still a good enough combat simulator that the Marine Corps uses a modified version of it (called Marine Doom) to teach recruits how to kill. They use it as a tactical training device, as opposed to teaching motor skills—although when used with a pistol grip joystick it has some value there, too. Its primary value is in developing the will to kill by repeatedly rehearsing the act until it feels natural.

It's safe to say that such technology is much more dangerous in the hands of kids than among soldiers and cops—these above examples prove that, as does common sense. There often are no safeguards at home and in arcades, no supervision, nor anyone around to put this technology into perspective for a child. In the military and law enforcement worlds, the right option is often not to shoot, and recruits receive extensive training about this. Often, recruits are reprimanded, punished, or even "failed" and kicked out for making too many mistakes—that is, for shooting the wrong targets. But when a kid puts his quarter in a video machine, there is *always* the intention to shoot. There is never an incentive not to shoot. And there's always some stimulus to keep excitement high, heart rate up, thinking functions closed down. This process is extraordinarily powerful and frightening. The result is ever more homemade pseudosociopaths who kill reflexively, even when they don't intend to.

The Duke Nukem series provides a good current example of just how gruesome and explicit the violence of the home video games has recently become. In this popular "shooter" game, the player is behind a weapon of choice, shooting everything in sight to get to the next level in order to shoot everything in sight. The "shooter," Duke, who is controlled by the player and looks somewhat like the Terminator, moves through pornography shops, where he finds posters of scantily clad women he can use for target practice. In advanced levels, bonus points are awarded for the murder of female prostitutes, women who are usually naked. Duke often encounters defenseless, bound women, some of whom are even conveniently tied to columns and plead, "Kill me, kill me."

A game called Postal takes the horror one step further. The user gets to "go postal" and receives points for killing as many innocent victims as possible while they beg for mercy. Likewise Redneck Rampage, where you can do the same with farm animals and farmers. The latest technology permits you to scan pictures of your fellow students and teachers from your high school yearbook and "morph" them onto the faces of the people you kill. Like many "First Person Shooter" games, Quake is often played with a joystick, which is really more like a pistol grip complete with trigger, that lets the child point (and thereby move the gun on the screen) and shoot (by pulling the trigger, which causes the gun on the screen to fire and recoil). Then there is House of the Dead, in which you blow away chunks of the bodies you fire at and get clean kills only for head shots; and CarnEvil, where you fire a pump-action shotgun and learn how to handle that skill. A new game on the market, Kingpin: Life of Crime, is raising a lot of eyebrows due to its heightened realism and level of violence. Experts are saying it makes other current games look like B movies. For example, a player can shoot a character in fifteen different places "and see the damage done—including exit wounds"; the game comes with a sound track from the popular rap group Cypress Hill; and your "enemies" like to remind you that they'll "kick your ass." One ad for the game's release is drawing a lot of fire from parental watchdog groups. It says: "You're Gonna Die."

It's interesting to note that the makers of games like Kingpin assiduously deny that their game is meant for kids or marketed to that group. Indeed, many such games carry warnings and are labeled for a "mature" audience, and they do have increasingly large adult followings. But deny it or not, these games (the word itself suggests that the core audience is young) easily get into the hands of kids. The makers of the games, distributors, store owners, and parents are not exactly as vigilant about stopping children from buying them as they would be if we were talking about, say, cigarettes or pornography. "Unfortunately, video games are stuck with the kiddie label," said Gary Eng Walk in an article in *Entertainment Weekly*, "and everyone . . . tends to drop their guard when letting the rough stuff find its way to the under-seventeen crowd." He's right, up to a point. It's hard to deny that many video game producers have actively sought out the "kiddie" label for their products. Obviously, we can't lump all games together, but it's impossible not to see the blatant marketing to children that is going on at all levels. The language of the ads, the highly effective packaging, the million-dollar promotion campaigns are all aimed at fairly young audiences. Either that or extremely immature adults. It's worth noting that the aforementioned Duke Nukem 3-D is available at toy stores. In many toy stores the ultraviolent video games are not in a different area, hidden from innocent eyes. In fact, the larger stores arrange their video games alphabetically. Duke Nukem, rated M for mature audiences, seventeen and older, is shelved next to Eggs of Steel, a kiddie game about an animated egg. Duke action figures, which are becoming popular with boys eight years old and younger, can be ordered on-line.

The gaming industry can talk all they want about the age groups they're aiming their products at, but the truth is that if ratings were strictly enforced, they would lose countless young consumers. It's no mystery that most people don't even know a rating system exists—it's hard to tell. Even Doug Lowenstein, of the Interactive Digital Association, admits there is a problem. "[The ratings system] simply doesn't have the visibility and the awareness it should have," he says. "When you talk to everyone from reporters to politicians, and these people think there isn't a system, then it tells you that you have work to do." Indeed.

Leafing through any game magazine can be an eye-opener. "Fatalities can be the best part of Mortal Kombat." (Mortal Kombat action toys are labeled "For children four and up.") A new game for your child's enjoyment is "as easy as killing babies with axes." Another one is "more fun than shooting your neighbor's cat." Capcom's latest Street Fighter proclaims, "The killer in me is just beginning." Robert Lindsey, head of sales and marketing for the U.S. unit of Japan's Capcom, acknowledges that teenagers are an important audience: "I refer [to] them as my early adapters—if I get them on board, I know I'll get everyone else."

The on-line availability of violent video games is a big part of the problem. Label first-person shooter sites with any warning you want, there's still really nothing to stop a kid with access to a computer from seeing what's there, communicating with other players, and ordering an array of products. In fact, warnings can serve the opposite purpose; most kids we know see them not as a caution but as an advertisement. They want the game to be more violent, more adult. It gives the product validity. Kids have to get past the manned ticket counter to see restricted films; they have to provide proper identification that they are old enough to buy cigarettes and alcohol; but there are no such obstacles in their way if they want to learn all there is to know about Kingpin and other "mature" video games.

So with all the evidence to suggest that these games are dangerous—that they're modeled after military killing simulators, that they are superviolent and graphic, that the user is rewarded for killing, and that kids are playing with these games way too often and for too long—it is particularly egregious that they are being marketed to kids, and marketed in ways that highlight all that is bad for them. What kind of message does this send? Well, yet another on-line ad for Kingpin gives us a pretty good indication: "The Creators of Redneck Rampage are about to bring you a new, urban drama that finally proves that crime pays." As we ourselves tolerate these games and even label them fun, we are also telling our children that slower-paced, less emotionally arousing screen fare is boring. Arouse instead of awaken; excite instead of examine; splatter instead of study—this is what we're telling them. And they're listening.

5

DON'T JUST
STAND THERE...
DO SOMETHING!

We are both parents—five sons in total—so we know firsthand the incredible challenges of raising kids in the latter part of the twentieth century. We also realize that instructing children to "just turn off" violent programming in all its forms, or "just say no" to drugs, alcohol, and premarital sex, doesn't address how complicated these issues are or the circumstances in which children face them. Although the "just turn it off" option can be part of an overall solution, it is becoming nearly impossible for kids, especially, to do so because of the proliferation of media entertainment outside the home and the peer pressure they encounter daily.

We are talking to more and more parents of all ages (and with all ages of children) who know that most of what their kids are watching and playing is not good for them. The problem is that they don't know how to tackle the issue in any meaningful way. The best intentions are great, but without practical, usable solutions, they may not make much difference. Whether their children are in their first years and are only starting to be exposed to violent entertainment, or are much older and have been exposed to it for a while, parents are feeling outmanned in this war. The size of the entertainment behemoth, the impact it has on children at all levels, and its obvious lack of restraint when it comes to airing violence, be it in movies, on television, or in video games, have grown at a bewilderingly rapid rate. Add the fact that kids are spending increasingly inordinate amounts of their time watching slasher films and playing games like Doom, and many of us just throw up our arms and surrender. Well, don't. Keeping parents, teachers— everyone—from raising the white flag is our whole reason for writing this book. Educating our children and shaping them into functioning, levelheaded adults must always be within our grasp. Educating ourselves on this issue is the best place to start.

That said, we can focus on the fact that as parents we do have a lot of influence and authority. It's knowing how to use our position that can make all the difference with our kids—and on the impact of the violence they absorb.

It's important to remember that children of different ages and stages of development need slightly different rules and guidelines. The younger the child, the more important it is to protect him or her against all forms of violence in entertainment. As children develop literacy skills, higher-level thinking abilities, and more self-monitoring and self-calming capabilities, they are better equipped to discuss violent imagery, understand its impact, and, ultimately, deal with it more effectively. This is what we think all parents want for their children—the ability to respond thoughtfully to sensational, glamorized portrayals of violence. And for that to happen, it means we have to become very involved, right from the beginning.

The big question is: How do we protect our kids and at the same time empower them to know what's going on? Or, put slightly differently, how do we protect their best interests without smothering them in the process? Start by remembering a few guidelines.

First, dealing effectively with media violence in the home is a *process*. If your kids have seen more than you would have liked them to—if you think they may be lost causes—take action anyway, knowing that steps you take now to remedy the situation will pay huge dividends in the long run. If you are new parents and want to know how to get started with your baby, begin by understanding that your ideal may not always be obtainable— we all run into stumbling blocks, and it's not the end of the world. We have heard many colleagues who are child development specialists, doctors, psychologists, and media literacy professionals lament the amount of time their own children spend in front of the TV, or the way their kids are enamored with Hulk Hogan or with playing Duke Nukem. The point is, you can read all the pertinent studies, do everything in your power to keep violent programming at bay, and have a wonderful, loving relationship with your kids, and they'll still probably go through phases that seem a little scary to you. So it's important to remind ourselves that we, as parents, are in it for the long haul. It's the cumulative effects of our consistent attitudes, actions, and values that will educate our children, not a few isolated incidents.

Second, we want to stress the notion of *perception*. How do your kids perceive your stance on media violence? Children, as we have demonstrated, imitate what they see and are very affected by their surroundings. And if they don't see and hear you condemning abject, graphic screen violence, they will not comprehend why it's bad for them. They're taking their cues from you, so make it clear that violence in all its forms is unacceptable. Very young children need to hear statements like: "If people truly cared about kids they wouldn't put that on for you to watch." "You are not old enough to understand that show, so we are going to switch to another station. Let's see what else is on that will teach you good things." Older children and teens are hungry for your guidance and input, even though they take pains to act otherwise. Still, it's often hard to sit them down and discuss violent screen images without having them think you are cramping their style. But it can be done. Suggest watching movies at home together; compare older films with violence (*Patton, Ben Hur,* for example) to newer films (such as *Die Hard 2*) and discuss the differences; chat about why certain kinds of entertainment are offensive and belittling to their audiences. As we share our perceptions with our kids, they become more perceptive—it's that simple.

Our third point has to do with *power*. How can we help our children feel powerful so they don't need to feed off the pseudo-power of, say, a Teenage Mutant Ninja Turtle? Authentic power has nothing to do with physical force, domination, coercion, or inflicting suffering. As we help a child acquire a quiet, inner knowing of self-confidence and self-respect, TV thugs or video game madmen become less glamorous and more inane. Kids do possess a natural fascination with physical power, so why not steer them in a better direction by letting them study a martial art? Many martial arts instructors are excellent role models for teaching power and knowing the right time and place to use it. Other parents have found that when their kids develop a talent in music or art, they are more self-reliant and less screen-enamored. There are myriad ways we can build a child's confidence and sense of empowerment, and once that has been accomplished we're halfway there.

It's always a good idea to sit down with your kids and discuss the misuse of power in violent screen portrayals. As we've said, the worst kind of screen violence, the most reckless and irresponsible use of it, is when it is stylized, graphic, and there's no sense of real aftermath to the action. Children and teens both need to be continually reminded that those who are feeling small, afraid, weak, and helpless are often the first to resort to violence. And no matter how good it looks on-screen, how cool it makes the perpetrator seem, it's important for kids to understand the difference between domination over someone and control of a situation or event; that a powerful person is one who knows they always have a choice—the choice to harm or the choice to help.

Finally, keep *perspective* on the situation. One divorced mother we know found out that her kids were watching all kinds of violent fare every weekend when they spent time at their father's house. She was very concerned about the situation and didn't know what to do. Our advice was simple. Start by doing what you can and then work from there. This woman was doing all the right things at her house and she did have custody of her children five out of seven days. But she made sure she carved out time with them and paved the way for discussing the issue of violent entertainment. The children were ages eight and ten when she began this "ritual," and she invited them to discuss what they watched on television at their dad's. The floodgates opened. They were consumed with what they took in on their weekend visits but knew it wasn't all good, clean fun. But like a lot of kids, they had no framework in which to discuss what they saw. Their mother talked with them, asked them questions, modeled appropriate reactions, and encouraged them to think and question everything they saw. Her children are now well-adjusted young adults with keen insights into the human condition far beyond their years. The lesson here is: don't overreact and don't ever think the game is lost.

These guidelines offer a solid framework in which to work with your children to lower their intake of violent programming and game playing. The following hints get down to the nitty-gritty of everyday life—collectively, call them a blueprint for action on the home front.

ESTABLISH A FEW RULES AND STRIVE FOR CONSISTENCY

Until the entertainment industry gets it, either by legislative force, parental pressure, or some epiphany on their part, it's basically up to us to set boundaries for our children concerning violent entertainment. So where to start? The average American child watches four hours of television each day through the most formative years, until age eighteen. So let's start here, by decreasing the amount of time your child spends in front of the television; for when we do that we also decrease the chances of kids running into inappropriate content in the first place. We realize that reducing the amount of viewing time is perhaps the toughest part of this equation, but you'll get results. Moderate viewers who watch one or two hours of television a day are much more likely to have other areas of interest and be more successful in school than are heavy viewers. So the bottom line as advised by the American Academy of Pediatrics is to reduce all screen time (including TV and arcade video games, handheld video games, and computers, along with TV and video) to one or two hours a day. (There are those families that are adopting a "no television" policy with their children and getting good results. Although this is not a viable solution for many parents, and we're not saying that television is completely devoid of good programming for children, completely cutting out television from a child's diet is working for some.)

Here are some tips to making this goal a reality: Ensure that kids finish their homework before they watch television; use a timer to indicate when video game or computer play must end; create a "budget" of ten hours of screen time weekly—and enforce it. As well, make time on the weekend to sit down as a family and figure out what the kids will watch during the upcoming week. Will a TV program or a video rental be something you want to use while you get dinner on the table some nights? Can you count on these programs or videos to be safe? Let the kids make decisions based on choices that you offer them; getting them involved in the process of choosing when and what they will watch will reinforce healthy TV and video habits. With this practice they will learn over time to monitor their own viewing and playing habits.

It's especially important to note that if a child is experiencing difficulties such as behavior or learning problems or hyperactivity, overuse of TV and video games usually exacerbates the problem, taxing parental patience and adding to the child's stress. In cases such as these, the less screen time the better.

Another area that parents can concentrate on is the physical placement in the home of the television set and/or computer. Needless to say, we strongly suggest to parents that their children not have television sets in their bedrooms. We think the same when it comes to computers. Of course, there are exceptions, especially with computers, as their use pertains to learning and homework, but it really is best in most cases to avoid having children in front of either device without some kind of supervision. So put this electronic furniture in the family areas, where you can be around. You don't have to be hovering like a hawk all day and night, but it will certainly be harder for kids to spend hours a day watching violent programming or playing point-and-shoot video games. And it will definitely be easier for you to be part of the process.

A lot of people ask us about the V-chip. Can that help you set boundaries? Well, yes and no. You can block violent content, but determining what material to block may get a little confusing. You can't really rely on the TV ratings system. According to the 1998 report "State of Children's Television," which examined 1,190 shows across broadcast, cable, and public television, 75 percent of children's shows containing three or more malicious acts of violence carried no indicator of violence, such as the FV label for "fantasy violence." According to the report, the inconsistencies leave parents using the V-chip with a no-win situation.

BUILD CHILDREN'S LANGUAGE AND READING SKILLS

The best way to counter a negative is with a positive. So help your children to become articulate readers and writers. A well-developed language system gives the brain a well-developed mental function. Since the prefrontal cortex is an important component in dampening impulsive, aggressive behavior, children and teens with strong language abilities and problem-solving skills are more apt to be able to control themselves.

Some researchers believe that literacy skills actually prevent violent behavior. Consider this observation by Dr. Bruce Perry, the director of CIVITAS Child Trauma Programs at Baylor College of Medicine and Texas Children's Hospital:

> A striking example of the role of cognitive development (development of a literate population) on violence comes from historical accounts of violence. In the year 1340 in Amsterdam, the murder rate was in excess of 150 murders per 100,000 people. Two hundred years later the murder rate was below 5 per 100,000 people. Clearly this is not a genetic phenomenon. The genetics of the population of Amsterdam likely did not change much in two hundred years. This marked decrease in the incidence of murderous violence is likely due to the development of a higher percentage of individuals in that society having better developed cortices—more capable of abstract cognition, and thus more capable of modulation of aggressive and violent impulses. The

sociocultural phenomenon underlying the development of healthier and more capable cortices was, without question, literacy. The introduction of the printing press allowed the percentage of literate (i.e., cortically-enriched, cognitively capable) individuals to dramatically increase. Over a few generations, the impact of a number of bright, abstract individuals transformed their society.

This is not to say that smart, literate people do not commit crimes, but they do commit fewer than others. It should give us pause when we consider how many millions of adults in America are functionally illiterate.

It may sound like a simple solution—too simple to be believable—that literacy skills can act as a buffer to potentially violent behavior. But the more a child is able to verbalize and think on higher levels, the easier it will be to teach children about consequences of violence. In addition, literacy skills give kids a profound edge in coming to terms with screen portrayals of violence. A rich vocabulary along with know-how at self-expression gives kids essential tools for articulating feelings, opinions, and ideas about media violence that a less literate child does not have.

Parents hear this mantra from teachers often, but we cannot stress it enough: Read aloud to your child. This is so important, especially in a culture where the visual image has replaced listening to language. The more TV that is watched in the home, the less conversation there is. A recent Canadian study demonstrated that 40 percent of parents could not remember a time when they ate their evening meal with the TV off! And an American study has shown that 82 percent of parents of elementary school–age children do not encourage reading at home. This is way off track. If we want to help our children grow minds that can resist and understand media violence, we need to make language activities a family priority. Turn off the TV and talk and read.

When children and teens are watching TV they are usually not talking, and thus are not learning to express themselves or their ideas. They certainly are not reading and exercising their imaginations. And although they are listening to words spoken on the screen, most of what they listen to are sound bites lacking enough linguistic complexity to build their language abilities. Also, salient visual images often get in the way of paying much attention to the language. When children under research conditions watch a TV program whose audio track differs from its visual images, many times what they remember as the "story" is the visual display. TV also can't respond to the child; it can't ask or answer a question or repeat or slow down or stop to give the child time to absorb what's being said. And much of the time the images are coming in faster than the child can thoughtfully process them. The more violent the program, the more fast-paced it will be. One of the more depressing sights for us is the look of a child in front of the TV as he or she watches hours of mindless, pointless violence (or even mindless and pointless nonviolent drama or comedy). They look catatonic; they seem to register little or nothing, as if their small brains are being fried, which is similar to what's happening.

Pictures on the screen are immediately accessible. As Dr. Russell Harter, a major researcher in the area of children and literacy, points out, "Television . . . is not very symbolic. . . . It makes things easy to understand." Language, though, in any form, whether it be print, sound, Braille, or sign language, is basically symbolic. It is a representation of concepts and thoughts whose meaning must be unlocked by the workings of the cerebral cortex. Watching pictures on the screen does not in and of itself require mental gymnastics, especially for children's developing brains. It is only when conversation is added—a question is asked or a comment given—that the child develops the cognitive structure to make sense of the images. A TV in the house doesn't necessarily mean that family members will stop talking to each other. But unless adults intentionally engage children in conversation about what's coming across the screen, children can grow up to prefer passive viewing to active thinking while they watch. When it's violence they're watching, the effects can be devastating.

Children at any age can be captivated by a story on audiotape. Most teens will enjoy listening to a classic such as the *Lord of the Rings* trilogy—about twelve hours of mental gymnastics! Young children can learn to operate their own tape recorders and listen to twenty- to thirty-minute story tapes, readily available at libraries. As kids take in language without too many accompanying pictures, they must make up the pictures in their own minds. Even if we read a beautifully illustrated book out loud, there may be twenty or so pictures. But not every picture is given, as is the case with TV programs or movies. A daily practice of family time where books are shared and discussed goes a long way toward helping children develop both logical, sequential thinking patterns and metaphoric muscles capable of imaginative thought.

DISCUSS THE PRODUCTION TECHNIQUES USED TO MAKE VIOLENCE SEEM "COOL"

A basic notion that children need to understand as early as possible is that all media is intentionally constructed for specific audience reactions. Nowhere could this be truer than for violent entertainment. We are not advocating that you show violence to your children, but rather, when they do happen to see it, you can point out the production techniques that make it so appealing. For instance, demonstrate how background music makes the action seem thrilling, as does slow motion; show them how a close-up of a gun to someone's head plays on strong emotions such as terror; help kids understand how much the producer, director, video game designer wants to draw in an audience.

Years ago, a movie critic pointed out how the difference in point of view in horror films spoke volumes. Almost always, when the camera's point of view was the villain's or monster's, the film was sadistic, gratuitous, and of little or no value other than invoking terror in its audience. Explain this to kids; help them deconstruct on-screen violence and let them see the strings attached and why and how they're being pulled. In a sense, the emperor has no clothes, and by pointing out and talking about all the tricks and special effects, we help demystify violent imagery for kids.

The same goes for violent video games, but we're up against a bigger problem with that technology. For one thing, the whole game world is more shut off from adults than are television and movies. It's not really on our radar. We make a practice of flipping channels, going to movies, renting videos, but you won't find too many parents in video arcades or hunched over Play-Stations. What makes video games potentially more dangerous to children is that they can create their own reality with these interactive toys—it's them and the action, no distractions. Still, take an interest in this technology. Try to sit down and play the games with your children. Point out how often women are placed in victim positions; how the pace is fast to keep you hyped up; that shooting a target over and over again is not a particularly great way to spend one's money and time. For your own sake, pick up a gaming magazine like *PC Gamer* and check out the ads. See what you're up against: "Gratuitous Violence Is 200 Times Faster with a D-Link Network"; "No Cure. No Hope. Only Death"; "Destroying Your Enemies Isn't Enough . . . You Must Devour Their Souls." Parents we know had no idea this stuff even existed, and we can tell you that their jaws dropped when they watched, played, and read about what's going on in the video game industry today. But it spurred them to act, and it put them on more equal footing with their kids when it came time to talk about it.

As we explain what's happening behind the scenes, kids will be less likely to take what's happening in front of them too seriously. Even very young children can be taught the concept of authorship. They hear about authors of books, but not usually about scriptwriters for violent cartoons. With teens we can remember that they like to test, question, and poke around with new ideas.

Kids don't like to be seen as the fool, either. They aren't naturally thinking through the violence-as-entertainment angle, but with a little encouragement from us, they may decide for themselves that screen violence is stupid, developed by adults to cater to the lowest common denominator and remove cash from wallets. Let's not underestimate their curiosity and adaptability, nor lower our expectations to the depths of the entertainment industry's expectations for our kids.

EXAMINE SENSATIONAL VS. SENSITIVE PORTRAYALS OF SCREEN VIOLENCE

The age and stage of development matters in the interpreting of visually violent images. If younger than eight, youngsters should not see any sensational, gratuitous violence—ever. As children become verbally able to express ideas and analyze information, they can learn to understand, discuss, and appreciate sensitive portrayals of violence that can teach empathy and respect for life. The shooting of the dog in the movie *Sounder* is an example of such violence. The dog, the movie's namesake, symbolizes the unity and love of the family. When it is shot, it whimpers and runs away (and will reappear later in the story, but you don't know that at the time). There is nothing gratuitous about this scene. A child watching it can learn about suffering and cruelty. It provides parents with a wonderful opportunity to discuss the consequences of hurting an animal or a person. It can be a catalyst for good.

The movie *Fresh* can do the same for teens. Although rated R, most likely for a few graphically violent scenes, the film shows realistic violence with a message. Yes, the violence is graphic. But the immense consequences of the violence for a twelve-year-old boy are also shown graphically. Violent acts exact high prices. Watched with a parent or caring adult, *Fresh* can give a fifteen-year-old a perspective on violence that can't be found in shoot-'em-up action adventure flicks or the latest high-tech thriller. More of these types of movies need to be made—films that parents can watch with teens and then discuss afterward, that show the human condition in all of its ugliness, but show it sensitively, without fanfare, and devoid of special effects. The response the producers obviously want to provoke is that viewers walk away shaking their heads in disgust at the villains and the harm they caused.

Most kids can't reach that level of response when violence is portrayed as glamorous. In fact, with all the sensationalistic splatter available to our kids on TV, in movies, and in video games, the only normal reaction they can have is to think it's cool to kill someone. We have discussed this previously, and it's important for parents to be aware of the differences between sensational and sensitive portrayals of violence. There are characteristics for both that are easily detected. Sensational violence features lots of action, fast-paced filming, and tons of special effects. The killing looks like fun, the perpetrator has little or no remorse for what he's done, and in the end there are no consequences. You as the viewer walk away psyched up, thrilled, feeling good. Characteristics of sensitive portrayals of violence shouldn't give you that high. Entertainment like this is more slow-moving, with more dialogue, to provoke thinking as well as feeling; the violence, and there's no need to show too much of it, should upset you and elicit compassion for what you've seen. There should be no suggestion that the suffering, murder, and mayhem is fun.

We all know the differences between good and bad portrayals of violence, and we all know it's a battle to get kids interested in something more slow-paced and thoughtful when they are surrounded by entertainment that is just the opposite. But understand that we have a choice.

DEAL DIRECTLY WITH TV NEWS PROGRAMS

We haven't tackled violence on the TV news because it is quite different from the entertainment we have been discussing. Still, it's on-screen, it can be horribly graphic, and it can be used almost purely to keep audiences in place. Also, we shouldn't overlook the fact that overexposure to violence in the news can lead to a child seeking it out in entertainment. Much of what is covered on television news involves violence and the most negative aspects of human behavior. In fact, we as adults are often stunned by the number of bloody images and bad messages that fill the average half hour of news. We often come away from it wondering if anything good happens anywhere in our world. Although the networks would like to think that they are offering us a truly balanced version of what's happening around us, we all know that that is almost never the case. Just as in fictional entertainment, violent stories and accompanying images are often used on the news to manipulate the viewer. That said, letting children, especially very young children, watch the news on a regular basis can be very harmful to their worldview.

Preschoolers are definitely not ready to watch TV news. There is no news program written for the three- to five-year-old set. And there shouldn't be. The evening news offers too many displays of graphic violence that would be very difficult to explain to a young child. It is a mistake to even have the evening news on when preschoolers are around. As we have shown earlier, for the young child, images are alive—they have power. With children under age eight, parents might consider watching a later news program when the child is asleep, watching the news while a spouse or an older child plays with the younger child in another room, taping the news program to view later, or listening to radio news instead. Viewing news programs—ones without violent images—that are designed especially for children in the eight-to-ten-year range, such as Linda Ellerbee's *Nick News,* will keep them abreast of current events without the sensational violence. But, as with young children, there is no overwhelming reason they should see news shows produced for adults.

By age eleven or twelve, most kids will have developed the necessary language and thinking skills to analyze news programs designed for their age group. Many teachers use *CNN Newsroom and WorldView* to engage middle-school students in discussions about current events. Families can tape it and watch it at home, too, or kids can watch other news programs designed specifically for them. But be around; answer questions, ask questions, discuss the news, and help your kid put what he sees into context.

Younger teens and high school students can learn a lot from TV news if they know how to approach it. This can be a great starting point for discussing violent topics with them, providing an opportunity to expose teens to a broader view. For instance, a news report on youth gang violence provides the opportunity to discuss the realities and myths about youth violence. There are questions you can ask them, such as: Is this news story covering a violent crime important enough to take up two minutes of 40 million people's time? What do you think about what happened at Littleton, Jonesboro, Paducah? Do you really believe it's necessary to the validity of a story to repeatedly show violent, graphic images? Just as with violent entertainment, get them thinking, help them deconstruct what they see.

CHOOSE SLOWER-PACED, QUALITY SCREEN ENTERTAINMENT FOR YOUR CHILDREN

Slow down the pace of what kids watch. Select TV programs, videos, and video games that have a slower pace and require some thinking. Count the seconds between image changes. If each image changes rapidly, every two or three seconds, the pace is too quick. With image changes that vary in length, children have time to digest what they are seeing and will be conditioned to interact with what they watch rather than merely react to quick impressions.

By providing more slow-moving programs and videos for children, we are reducing their exposure to gratuitous violence, because quick pacing usually means more violent content. A movie or a TV program slow enough to be thought-provoking will probably be nonviolent or less sensationally violent. This isn't a steadfast rule, but it is true in most cases.

Also, our kids want quality. Educational, informational television programs are identified by the label E/I. An important study indicated that children are not turned off by this identification. In fact, 40 percent of ten- to seventeen-year-olds said they would be more likely to watch such a program. This was double the number who said they would be less likely to watch. Seek out entertainment for your child that depicts human diversity, contains sensitive portrayals of suffering and the human condition, reflects your family's values, supports your goals for your child, enhances your child's understanding of self and others, and inspires and encourages prosocial behaviors and attitudes.

REFUSE TO BUY OR CONDONE VIOLENT VIDEO GAMES

The trend of giving video games to toddlers, preschoolers, and elementary school children must stop. Even if parents are introducing only nonviolent video games at this stage of development, it is going to be so much more difficult to keep the kids away from violent ones. Just the nature of video games in and of themselves make them potentially addictive. Video game systems are just not developmentally appropriate for children. The concept of timeliness needs to resurface and take main stage here. What is important and timely at one stage of a child's development can be a disaster at another stage.

Children do not need video games and, in fact, the earlier they are introduced in a child's life, the more likely it is that the child will crave violent ones within a short time. Parents can make it so much easier on themselves by encouraging slower-paced computer games until the child's mental habits are set, usually somewhere around ages twelve to fourteen. The introduction of video games then will be less likely to lead to stimulus addiction and the urge for violent video games as thrill-providing devices. And there are choices: If your child has a predilection for video games at this age, we urge you to read up on and think about buying those games that do not contain gratuitous violence, those that challenge your child to think critically and creatively, and that require perseverance through a mentally challenging problem. There are games that serve as jumping-off points for further study, hobbies, or educational pastimes, games that don't require marksmanship and an ability to shrug off carnage and killing. We have a hard time recommending any type of noneducational video game, but certainly the sports games on the market—such as basketball, baseball, car racing, or golf—are preferable to anything with violence in it.

Does such a tactic sound radical? Parents who have taken this advice thank us profusely for the changes they see in their children. Of the hundreds of parents we know who introduced video games to their children when the kids were pre-teens or older, not one of these children became enamored by violent video games. Sure, they played them at friends' houses, even rented some and played them at home. But the overwhelming consensus after they found out what these games were about was: "These are stupid. All you do is go around shooting people. What's fun about that?" As incredible as this may sound, these kids preferred sports games and other types of games that provided a mental challenge. Why? They were not conditioned to kill during the most formative time of their brain development. Rather, their minds (and hearts) received the proper nourishment at the right times. Results were as expected: Thinking, well-functioning kids who found violence distasteful. In other words, normal children.

LISTEN TO YOUR CHILD

Listen to what your children are saying about violence. How are they interpreting it? One mother was overwhelmed when her son said, "I want to kill myself." Why wouldn't she be? She later realized that he was equating "self" with an action figure in a video game he had been playing regularly. Her little boy just parroted what he had been exposed to and failed to understand what he was really saying. However, that should be a clear demonstration to his mom that something is amiss.

In an article about the process of healing in a violent world, author Beverly Robertson Jackson tells this rather disturbing story of a concerned mother:

> I took my two-year-old son, Tim, on a field trip with his older brother, and he experienced an unexpected traumatic reminder. As we boarded the bus for the field trip, Tim went into hysterics. Because he was just beginning to talk, it was not easy to understand the nature of his terror. After calm coaxing he uttered the word "Kuger." The other children informed me that he thought the man across the aisle was Freddy Krueger.... Although Tim had never seen a horror movie, he had seen television commercials advertising such movies. In addition, he had not seen or interacted with many White males in his short lifetime. Thus he generalized his fear of Freddy Krueger to this encounter.

These are warning signs, and they should be warning parents of what their children are all about. Kids are not great at masking their emotions, so if your child is saying things about violence that give you pause, pick up on it and act accordingly. With this in mind, it is rather astonishing to think what Dylan Klebold and Eric Harris, the two boys who went on a killing rampage in Littleton, were doing right under the noses of their parents. They played hundreds of hours of the video game Doom, set up a racist Web site, built pipe bombs in the garage, armed themselves to the teeth with semiautomatic weapons, and talked to almost anyone who would listen about how they wanted to kill. Was anyone listening? Fifteen lives may have been saved if there had been.

Confront peer pressure

Peer pressure is perhaps our biggest stumbling block to getting kids on the right track, and this is true with almost everything bad for them. One new father we know despaired that any of his efforts to keep his child away from video games and on-screen

violence would result in the boy being an outcast with his classmates. It's hard to come to school and be one of the only kids who
haven't seen *RoboCop* or played Doom or watched every episode
of *Buffy the Vampire Slayer*. Kids want to fit in, and they see this
as one major way of doing that. What we as parents must do is
teach them not to play that game—not to care so much about
what their friends think that it controls their tastes and what they
want to do with their time. You'd be surprised at how little peer
pressure really matters, especially with kids under the age of thirteen, once parents actually try to do something about it.

Children are extremely adaptable. If we take a stand in our
homes, children respect that. The "Everyone else gets to watch it"
or "Everyone else plays those games" arguments can be coun-
tered by explaining that in your home you do things certain ways
for certain reasons. Your child may resist at first, but many parents we know have found that to their surprise, the kids give up
the battle to be "like everyone else" and acquiesce to parents'
standards.

The developmental tasks during childhood revolve around
building a strong self-identity and social skills. If children are
excluded from social interactions because they don't know the
latest media-violent enabler in the form of a toy, TV program,
movie or video game, their world does not collapse. They don't
lose face. In fact, they usually learn valuable lessons and gain the
respect of their peer group.

What parents need to focus on is not so much whether the
child is missing out on a culturally induced childhood "neces-
sity," but rather on building the child's sense of identity and
resiliency. If all parents started addressing this problem, our kids
wouldn't have nearly as much problem with peer pressure. Peer
groups would take their cues about what's important from
parental values, not from hawkers of violent media.

Take special care with young teens. From about ages eleven to sixteen, kids want to be like their peers and around their peers as much as possible. Parental influence takes a backseat. What we have instilled up to this point in a child's life almost seems to go underground, fermenting somewhere in the depths, but not clearly visible. Have a look at the advertising of certain violent films, TV shows, and, especially, video games, and you'll see that it zeroes right in on this age group's isolation, rebelliousness, and sense of powerlessness. This stuff is not easy for parents to contend with when trying to get through to their kids.

Parents need to pick all of their battles, including those that pertain to their teenagers' viewing and playing habits. Parents who have had success dealing with peer pressure at this age have found themselves making compromises: "I won't let you go see *Scream* with your friends, but remember, I am letting you stay overnight at Pete's tomorrow night." "No, I am still blocking MTV, but I did buy you that CD I wasn't so crazy about." "As I keep telling you, I won't buy violent video games, but I will upgrade your system so you can get better sports games." If we link the "no" with a "yes," chances are their arguments will be shorter and we will win the important battles.

Peer pressure has been an excuse for kids since the beginning of time. We wouldn't let our kids buy guns if they said everyone had one; we wouldn't let them deal drugs because their friends did; and we wouldn't let them jump off the Brooklyn Bridge even if it was all the rage. So we absolutely should not let down our guard when it comes to watching and playing graphically violent fare. Abstaining won't kill our kids, or anyone else.

We would never be so arrogant or reckless as to suggest that it's easy to keep impressionable kids' heads on straight as they face a barrage of very violent programming and video games. It's not easy. The above recommendations are at least a start, though (see the Resources for more information). If nothing else, we hope that they empower parents in this issue, letting them know that there are things that can be done right in the home to lessen the effects that violence as entertainment has on kids. We also hope that parents understand that there are no hard-and-fast rules here, except that an enlightened, intelligent, and loved child is our best defense against rising youth crime rates.

Moving from the home front, let's have a look at the public barometer regarding this issue, and what we can do to push forward. As important as it is to effect change in your own children, it's also key to know where we stand in the fight against those segments of the entertainment industry that are peddling violence. We need to empower kids, but we also need to empower ourselves if we are to make a difference.

As sad as it is that it took a tragedy like the incident in Littleton to wake America and the world up from their collective sleep regarding the issue of violent entertainment, much good has happened since that awful day in April 1999. For one thing, there virtually isn't a newspaper, magazine, radio station, or TV station that hasn't run at least one story on the possible effects of on-screen violence on today's youth. The issue has taken a front seat with the public in a way it never has before. Of course, there are people, many of them in the entertainment industry itself, who still deny that there is any plausible connection between violent programming and video games and the escalating rate of youth violence. But there are many more out there who have read the facts, seen the evidence, and know something is very wrong. Among them is President Clinton. In the wake of Littleton he made it a priority to address the issue, and for the time being he has been consistently vigilant about calling the entertainment industry on the carpet to accept some responsibility. God knows, he's up against some tough lobbies, but so were the people and politicians who took on the tobacco and automobile industries. Clinton has recently ordered the Federal Trade Commission and the Justice Department to look at whether the makers of violent television, movies, and video games are "improperly" marketing this violence to children. We'll see what comes of it, but it's a solid step forward.

Some entertainment companies aren't waiting for legislation. Disney, for example, has ordered all violent video games out of their numerous premises. Would that others would take the same initiative. Soon they may have no choice. But in the past, many in the entertainment industry have demonstrated only arrogance in the face of mounting public outcry over the issue, dragging in the First Amendment whenever it was convenient to protect their bottom line. They have consistently shifted the responsibility away from themselves and right in the laps of their audience. When confronted with allegations of negligence, their first response is invariably "It's the parents' responsibility to keep an eye on what their kids watch and play with." Yes, it is the parents' responsibility. But it is also the parents' responsibility to protect their kids from guns, tobacco, alcohol, pornography, drugs, and explosives. And in all of these areas the community at large helps parents in their struggle to do this. Our society has deemed that marketing and selling .44 Magnums, cigarettes, booze, X-rated films and literature, cocaine, and dynamite to children is illegal. Knowing this, and faced with what we've demonstrated on page after page of this book, we must ask why, in this one, vital area, parents should be left on their own. The answers we're all getting are not cutting it.

The entertainment industry has gone out of its way over the years to convince us that their violent programming and games are really just good, clean fun. Incidents in Littleton, Paducah, and Jonesboro, for example, give us good reason to doubt that logic. Just turning on the television or playing a video game or two does the same. "We wouldn't sell it if people didn't buy it" is another favorite response. This is pimp logic. Drug dealer logic. Except that even pimps and drug dealers generally won't try to market to small children, and they don't claim a constitutional right to sell their products to our kids. Surely these "guardians of the public airwaves," an industry that markets products to children, can be held to a higher moral standard than this.

We've demonstrated how we can effect change in the home, but we must also be vigilant about getting the entertainment industry to own up to their end of the responsibility, just as the tobacco industry had to respond to the effects their product has on people. There are several ways to accomplish this, all of them effective.

We must start by educating parents on a national level. Like the campaign to convince Americans to "buckle up," or the campaign to warn us against the dangers of drunk driving, there must be an educational campaign, on the TV, in ads, in print media, everywhere, to inform parents of the potential harm associated with exposing kids to media violence. We've made some headway in the last few years, but there are just too many parents who are still completely uninformed about the issue. Even the tobacco and alcohol industries accept the need for warning labels on their products, and it is time for the TV, movie, and video game industries to rise up to at least this moral standard. The warnings, when there are warnings, and the rating systems on all of this material are not enough as they now exist. They are also not that truthful.

Most adults know that there are things they can have but their kids can't. Many adults smoke a cigar, drink a beer, shoot a gun, drive a car, or have sex; but they all recognize that these things are not desirable for their children. Now they need to begin to understand that violence, whether it is "professional wrestling" or *Natural Born Killers* or the video game Postal, is another product that may be okay for them but is potentially harmful for their kids.

Education about media and violence does make a difference.

Individuals of all walks of life, from judges to mothers, can begin to take effective action once they understand the role of screen violence in fostering and feeding violent crime. For example, a juvenile court judge in Florida, after hearing the facts on this issue, is now including in his sentencing such things as: community service at animal control centers, humane societies, and hospices to give youthful offenders some personal experience of death; removal of all point-and-shoot games from the home—and prohibition from being in the presence of these at friends' homes, malls, and so forth; and no viewing of R-rated media. The point is, educating the public at large is a giant first step toward getting changes made.

Would we be content with "self-regulation" and "voluntary restraints" to prevent the alcohol, tobacco, gun, drug, or pornography industries from marketing their products to our kids or grandkids? No. Then why should we be content with voluntary restraints and self-regulation to limit the entertainment industry from marketing their violent products to our kids? Again, why, in this one industry, with this one product, should the rules be different?

Congress has already initiated legislation to curb children's access to explicitly violent movies and video games. In June 1999, legislation sponsored by Representative Henry Hyde of Illinois was designed to restrict violent material from being made available to minors, much as current law shelters them from obscene material. The legislation was defeated by a two-thirds majority, but this wasn't a bad performance considering that the legislation was appearing for the first time, on short notice, and having been opposed by such a powerful industry. Also, there is another scheme floating around the Senate called the "21st-Century Media Responsibility Act." This comprehensive bill, sponsored by Senator John McCain (R-Ariz.) and Senator Joseph Lieberman (D-Conn.), would require makers of music CDs, movies, and video games to share a similar rating system that suggests an appropriate age and description of content. If this bill passes, any retailers who sell "mature" games, CDs, and movies to minors will face $10,000 fines.

Under this kind of legislation, we would treat screen violence in much the same way that we treat sexually obscene material: adults can have access to it, but anyone who provides it to kids can be subject to prosecution. Many years ago, *Hustler* magazine reprinted a picture from *Soldier of Fortune* magazine showing a real soldier with his brains blown out. The caption said: "This is the real obscenity." (*Hustler* is another manufacturer that does not claim any "right" to sell their product to your kids; they accept restraints on their industry, but the TV, movie, and video game industries fall short of even the moral standard set by *Hustler*.) Not to defend pornographers, but when it comes to what constitutes obscenity, *Hustler* may just have a point. Sex— granted, not quite *Hustler*-style—will be a normal, healthy part of most adult lives, but there is no place in any life for violence. Just one single act of violence in a lifetime can destroy the lives of the victim and the perpetrator and their families. The ultimate obscenity may well be violence, and perhaps it is time for us to initiate legislation that recognizes this fact.

It has been said that the law is the best teacher. This means, for example, that the ultimate purpose of seat belt laws is to educate and inform citizens about something that is important to all of us. The possibility of getting a ticket is not what makes most people buckle up their kids; they do it because they love their kids and they want to protect them. But the existence of seat belt laws serves as a powerful means to educate citizens about their responsibilities. The very existence of the law shows that our whole society says this is the right thing to do. Similar legislation in the realm of screen violence can have the same effect.

Legislative initiatives do not have to happen in Washington.

Every city, county, and state in America has all the authority it needs to help parents in the struggle to protect their kids from the toxic effects of screen violence. For example, Mason City, Iowa, has embraced a plan by their mayor to rid the town of violent video games, vowing "zero tolerance" for these murder simulators.

Another approach to legislative initiatives is the 'R' means 'R' law. President Clinton has said: "I also want to challenge the owners of movie theaters and video stores, distributors—anyone at any point of sale—to enforce the rating systems on the products that you sell. Check the IDs, draw the line. If underage children are buying violent video games or getting into R-rated movies, the rating system should be enforced to put a stop to it." What he is asking for is really only common sense. Why bother having such systems and warnings in place if they are patently ignored by everyone? We check IDs for alcohol, tobacco, guns, pornography, and fireworks, and we fine retailers who fail to do so. President Clinton went on to say, "And if, as many of us suspect, there is still too much gratuitous violence in PG-13-rated movies, the rating systems themselves should be reevaluated." Indeed, the rating system we enforce has to be a good one; and this from the mouth of one of the most pro-Hollywood presidents we have ever had.

Colorado Attorney General Ken Salazar has recommended legislation "requiring businesses that sell or rent violent or graphic videos to set up zones limiting access to minors." In the wake of the Littleton shootings similar legislation has been initiated at state and local levels across America. Under such legislation, a sixteen-year-old cannot buy an R-rated movie, and a twelve-year-old cannot rent a PG-13 movie, without parental consent. And if you buy your child a ticket to the latest animated feature at the local multiplex, the theater owner has a responsibility to create an environment in which the child cannot accidentally or intentionally go next door and be exposed to a hard-core "slasher" film.

One legislative initiative, proposed in the state of Washington, is a tax on violent media. Our society determined, earlier in this century, that in America adults have a constitutional right to buy and drink alcohol. But the government also has a right to tax this product, and tobacco, and many other products, in order to recover some of the costs associated with the products' impact on society. Money is usually the incentive for pushing violent entertainment in all its forms; hitting back in the pocketbook would probably be very effective—and it would send out the message that these products are dangerous and do have consequences when sold to kids.

Another piece of legislation, proposed by two leading trial lawyers, is one establishing that media entities can be held accountable, in civil litigation, for the pain and suffering that can be linked to a specific source of media violence. We already do have this right, but state and federal legislation to this effect would be very useful. Jack Thompson, the attorney in the $130 million lawsuit against the media in the Paducah school shootings, states that such a statutory provision "would be the most powerful deterrent of all and not subject to prosecutorial will: creation of a tort claim by anyone suffering an injury at the hands of someone trained by a video game."

Civil litigation is really just another form of education. It is how we educate an industry. Because of our litigation system we have the safest cars and the best-trained cops in history. Lawsuits, or even the threat of them, help keep businesses and government from acting recklessly. So maybe one solution is to sue the makers of violent entertainment when it is clear that their product was in some way responsible for violence in the real world. They sell violence in order to make money. If they are full members of the marketplace, if they are going to take a profit, then the health of the society demands that they be fully liable to civil lawsuits, just like anyone else who provides a product or service in our nation. Is it easy to prove their complicity in most instances? No, and it never will be. But when a young boy, obsessed with point-and-shoot video games, obsessed with movies about young boys getting revenge on their classmates, picks up a real weapon for the first time and, with deadly accuracy, blows away a bunch of kids in school, it's probably safe to say that the makers of his obsessions have some real responsibility for his actions. That's what the families of Michael Carneal's victims are saying in Paducah with their lawsuit against the entertainment industry.

Ultimately, the only thing that rating systems in TV, movies, and video games have achieved is an admission from the entertainment industry that we need to protect kids from some of their products—and now this admission is being recognized. The FCC and the attorney general are investigating; they will have the option to subpoena the industry's secret files, and they can see if the industry has intentionally bypassed their own rating systems. If so, then they are clearly negligent and liable.

You see, in a free market our ultimate safeguard is civil liability. If you intentionally, negligently market a harmful product (alcohol, tobacco), and especially if you market it to kids (unsafe cribs, toys), then you will pay. Period.

The violent video games in particular, especially the ones where you hold a gun in your hand, will almost definitely not be found to have First Amendment protection, and that leaves them highly vulnerable. They are appliances, firearms trainers at best, murder simulators at worst. Even a book, *Hitman*, when its guidance and training was followed to commit real murders, was found by the Supreme Court to be subject to civil liability. If they are willing to hammer the written word (which clearly does fall under the First Amendment) when it teaches adults to kill, how can anyone possibly expect that children's access to these killing simulators will fall under the First Amendment?

In New York, a father taught his eight-year-old how to use and fire a gun. When the kid used that training to kill someone, the father was convicted of manslaughter. The father was using free speech to train his son, but what he trained the son to do was not acceptable by society, and he is now a convicted felon because of it. The extension of this legal process to the designers, manufacturers, and distributors of firearms trainers and murder simulators should be obvious.

It doesn't help their defense that the violent video game manu-facturers are selling their product to children as, literally, "killing simulators"—we described earlier their blatant advertising. How will they deny their own responsibility when a kid like Michael Carneal in Paducah uses what he's learned from their games to actually kill real humans? How will they defend themselves when a company like id Software licenses their product to the marines as a trainer, or when the army uses a slightly modified Super Nin-tendo system as a marksmanship trainer? They can't have it both ways. The concept of needing to protect children is completely embedded in science, law, and our culture. Any industry that tries to go against science, law, and culture is, quite simply, Doomed.

Another key reason to condemn the actions of that segment of the entertainment industry that markets violence is the simple fact that they have the option to market something other than violence. The alcohol, tobacco, and firearms industries by their natures have to market harmful products. That is, if they cannot sell alcohol, tobacco, or firearms, they cannot sell anything and must go out of business. But the video game industry can market nonviolent games (there are many good ones), and they can thrive and prosper without the violent games. They just choose not to do so. Often the representatives of the video game industry, in defense, claim that their major market is adults and that violent games are only a tiny fraction of their inventory. If that's true, then it would cost them very little to accept regulation in marketing violence to kids. And yet they fight, tooth and nail, any attempt to regulate the sale of violent games to kids.

These are two reasons (marketing to minors and viable alternatives) why those who peddle violence to kids, whether on TV, in movies, or in video games, are truly in deep trouble when they find themselves before American juries in product liability lawsuits. Those associated with the entertainment industry must stop trying to defend the indefensible, and recognize the direction in which the law is likely to go in this area. They should start doing what they can to protect themselves from the reasonable demands of society to seek redress against the people who helped to bring about violent criminal acts. That is probably why Disney pulled violent games from their hotels and theme parks, and why Walmart and Montgomery Ward have stopped selling violent video games, period. In the near future it will be extraordinarily expensive to get liability insurance for a business that designs, manufactures, or markets violent video games. That is what product liability lawsuits can accomplish.

The head of one state trial lawyers association believes that many media lawsuits have paid off for the plaintiffs. We just never hear about it because they settle out of court, paying the victims (or their survivors) large sums of money, once a month, for the rest of their lives, provided they keep their mouths shut. The only way to prevent this strategy of buying silence is to be sure that others know that victims have a right to their day in court. And that brings us back to education—the lawsuits are a message to the makers of violent entertainment, and to others who have suffered due to the industry's negligence.

The "death rattle," the last sound that leaves the body before death, is also a term that anthropologists use as a metaphor for an intense resistance to the obvious. Could it be that the purveyors of violent entertainment are hearing it? Dr. Jennifer James, an anthropologist and *Seattle Times* columnist, explains the phenomenon this way:

> Anthropologists who witness death and dying rituals report that many cultures believe they have to use rituals . . . to help the spirit move on to the next dimension, essentially helping the mind let go. . . . Our cultural and individual belief systems often do the same, intense resistance before transformation. If you think about the responses of some to civil rights in the 1960's or to women's rights, if you think about claims of tobacco manufacturers [or] producers of violent media . . . they all made or make the most absurd claims. . . . Whenever you encounter absurd rationalizations coupled with intense resistance, in yourself or others, the next move may be a letting go of the position once held so intensely. The noise, the death rattle, is the last effort to maintain a failing point of view.

One way that you, the citizen and parent, can speed this process is to give "fair warning" to businesses that market violence. If a mall, a store, or an arcade has adult violent video games, and if a movie theater creates an environment in which kids can get into R-rated films, then send them a letter about it. Talk to the manager and the owners and tell them that they will be subject to civil liability if they continue being negligent about enforcing restrictions. Discuss it with other parents. Certainly boycott the theaters and arcades until some action is taken.

And don't stop there. In the past few years, law students have brought about the release of prisoners from death row. They have, as part of their education, taken on the research and the legal steps to prove the innocence of several such prisoners. As part of their preparation for actually practicing law, these students have provided a socially significant benefit to society, both by freeing innocent prisoners and by calling attention to improper police tactics and practices.

What if groups of economics students at some institution such as MIT or the University of Chicago took on the task of identifying those corporations that benefited the most from selling violent entertainment to children? Their information could be posted on a Web site, exposing the company, the estimate of gross sales made on their violent products, the assumptions used in making the estimates, and so on. This could be an ongoing research project, perhaps updated quarterly or semiannually. There could be a Top 10 or Top 20 list of companies who benefit from selling violence to our kids. This information is out there somewhere as a part of the public record, but who knows about it? It needs to be teased out from a mountain of data somewhere and posted to focus public attention.

Most people don't understand that the FCC exists to serve us, not the industry. Phone Bill Kennard, the current chairman of the FCC, and ask him this question: Who owns "the airwaves"? He will have to admit that we, the people, do. What this means is that we have important influence. When we make a noise, it will be taken seriously. For instance, stations must provide quality educational programming for children or else they cannot get their licenses renewed. We can challenge stations at the local level in a way that is more difficult to do through a national organization. Just by picking up the phone and voicing concerns about what we are seeing (or not seeing) on our hometown channels, we can rattle cages enough to make important changes for our kids.

Anyone with a computer and some friends—or from the PTA

or a religious or service organization—and a bit of know-how can set up an E-mail group to start circulating information. People could send opinion pieces and letters of complaint en masse, voicing their joint concerns and demanding changes. Since it is very easy to set up collective mailing lists, in one evening, around a social event, the members of such a group could each send messages to the presidents and CEOs of entertainment companies, alerting them that there are concerned citizens out there who find on-screen violence marketed and sold to children offensive and wrong. At the same time, with the same keystroke, a copy of this message could be sent to senators and representatives, at both the state and federal levels. This would educate legislators about the will of their constituents.

Such action, multiplied on a national level, could mean several million E-mail messages received by the leaders of the entertainment industry in America, who would then only be lying to themselves when they claimed they were giving the people what they wanted. This would be several million E-mail messages to legislators, who would then have the backing to stand up to the special interest groups.

This is exactly the technique used by some very notable citizens to call for an entertainment industry "Code of Conduct." On July 21, 1999, former Education Secretary William J. Bennett and a bipartisan coalition of U.S. Senators unveiled on the Web (www.media-appeal.org) "a signed public appeal . . . calling on the entertainment industry to adopt a voluntary code of conduct to protect children and curb excessive media violence and sex." No less than Jimmy Carter, Gerald R. Ford, Colin Powell, Norman Schwarzkopf, Mario Cuomo, Steve Allen, Naomi Judd, and many other politicians and entertainers have signed the petition and strongly urged other concerned Americans to do likewise. The "Web petition" itself will reach millions—the news coverage about it will add to that number. While this group, admittedly, isn't your everyday collection of ordinary citizens, their method of calling attention to this issue can be adopted by anyone with Web access.

Media events are an excellent way of drawing attention to an issue. While a march on Capitol Hill would be one very powerful way to send politicians a message about violent entertainment, don't discount smaller events. Groups or individuals could sponsor gatherings in front of theaters or video game arcades to protest a new, particularly violent film or game that's been marketed to children. Or organize sit-ins at the offices of television stations, movie companies, and video game manufacturers. The point is, we have power as individuals and as groups, and we should take advantage of it.

The issue of violence in our culture, and the selling of violence to children for profit, needs to become a true national issue, where the voices of the parents, teachers, and child-care professionals are clearly heard by all, transcending the sound bites and the stonewalling of years past. The issue of media violence should become a part of the presidential race for the first presidency of the next century. In 1992, the leaders of President Clinton's successful campaign had a sign hanging on the wall for all to see, reminding them of what was key in the campaign: "It's the economy, stupid." What if, in the presidential campaign of 2000, the reminder became: "It's the violence, stupid"?

Remember the old saying "Insanity is doing the same thing over and over and expecting different results"? Have we been collectively insane over the past fifty years? If you flip through the Resources in this book and scan the chronology of research, congressional debates, and other documentation that has gone into attempting to deal with media violence since 1952, you should be outraged. How is it that millions of dollars and an uncountable amount of hours and energy have been put to work against TV, movie, and video game violence for decades . . . and things have only gotten worse? Screen violence has escalated beyond all sense of human civility and decency. Where does it end?

As we now reap the tragic harvest of our past impotence, we know in our minds and hearts that we cannot afford to go down the same road as before. We are now at an important crossroads, and so much of our children's future depends on what we do, or don't do, today. We have our marching orders: It is time for the people to lead. We cannot wait for legislatures to act. We cannot wait for judicial systems. And we certainly cannot wait for the entertainment industry to change course. Save for a few conscientious factions of that industry, the vast majority will have to be brought to their knees financially and in every other way before they'll stop teaching our kids to kill.

We have waited long enough. It is past time. It is time for each of us to take action, trusting that it will make a huge difference, because it will.

RESOURCES

A DEFINITION OF MEDIA VIOLENCE

The following is a definition of media violence. Not the only one, mind you, but one that we find gives fairly clear guidelines on a complicated issue. Let it act as a useful lens for viewing any type of entertainment or playing the hundreds of video games that exist on the market.

Violence is the intentional use of force to harm a human being or animal. Its outcome is injury—physical or psychological, fatal or nonfatal. It is true that violence is a part of the real world. However, we do not take our children to see autopsies performed as entertainment, nor do we invite someone into our living room to kill, brutally beat, or rape another person for our children to witness for their amusement.

Therefore, portrayals of violence in the media that glamorize and/or sensationalize violent acts toward other human beings or animals and show them as acceptable behavior provide a socially aberrant environment in which it is difficult to raise emotionally healthy children. Also, the prevalence of violence on television in itself imparts an implicit acceptability to the vicarious experience of violence and pushes the boundaries of cultural norms into the realm of social deviancy. From a synthesis of the research we find that harmful media violence includes:

- Plots that are driven by quick-cut scenes of gratuitous violent acts delivered in a rapid-fire frequency with graphic, salient technical effects.

- Graphic, sadistic revenge, torture techniques, inhumane treatment of others in a context of humor, trivialization, glibness and/or raucous "fun."
- Explicitly depicted violent acts shown through special effects, camera angles, background music, or lighting to be glamorous, heroic, "cool," and worthy of imitation.
- Depictions of people holding personal and social power primarily because they are using weapons, or using their bodies as weapons, and dominating other people through the threat of violence or through actual violence.
- Extraneous, graphic, gory, detailed violent acts whose intent is to shock.
- Violent acts shown as an acceptable way to solve problems or presented as the primary problem-solving approach.
- News programs that explicitly detail murder and rape, with information and graphic images not necessary for understanding the central message.

It should be noted, however, that any form of aggression on the screen has the potential to make children more aggressive. The more graphic and horrific the violence, the more likely the negative effects. Research clearly demonstrates that sensational media violence causes children and teens to become more aggressive and mean, creating fear, a lack of sensitivity to all forms of violence, and an increased appetite for violence—in real life and on the screen. An early preference for violent programming is a strong indicator of aggressive and antisocial behavior as an adult. Sensational portrayals, then, offer children a justification for violent acts in real life and perpetuate socially dangerous attitudes, behaviors, and values.

VOICES OF CONCERN
ABOUT ON-SCREEN
VIOLENCE

Throughout this book we have cited the work of many organizations that have contributed to the scholarship on the subject of violent entertainment and its negative effects on children. While we do not have the room to name every group that has commented on the issue, we present here a list of the major organizations—as well as how to contact them, and the specifics on the stands they take—that have set the tone and lent strong backing to our argument.

The American Medical Association (AMA)
515 North State St.
Chicago, IL 60610
312-464-5563
www.ama-assn.org

In 1952, an editorial in the *Journal of the American Medical Association* raised the topic of TV violence as a health issue. The editorial ran during the first Congressional hearings on the impact of television on delinquency.

At its 1976 meeting, the American Medical Association adopted a policy supporting research on the impact of TV violence. Also adopted at that meeting was a resolution that declared the AMA's "recognition of the fact that TV violence is a risk factor threatening the health and welfare of young Americans, indeed our future society."

In 1982, the AMA reaffirmed ". . . its vigorous opposition to television violence and its support for efforts designed to increase the awareness of physicians and patients that television violence is a risk factor threatening the health of young people."

In 1996, the AMA developed a guidebook for physicians with the goal of helping their patients understand the harmful effects of media violence. A portion of the summary in that guidebook reads:

"Television and other forms of visual media play an enormous role in everyday life, particularly in the lives of children and adolescents. While television serves in the education and socialization of children, there are also a number of health problems associated with the excessive watching of television, independent of content. In addition, an extensive body of research amply documents a strong correlation between children's exposure to media violence and a number of behavioral and psychological problems, primarily increased aggressive behavior. The evidence further shows that these problems are caused by the exposure itself. Physicians have important roles to play in diminishing children's involvement with violent media by serving as educators, advisors, and advocates. . . . There is an established body of evidence documenting the troubling behavioral effects of repeated exposure to media violence. . . . This guide offers physicians an overview of the health consequences of such exposure and how to understand the findings in relation to general societal violence, child development, and learning."

The American Psychological Association (APA)
750 First St. NE
Washington, DC 20002-4242
202-336-5500
www.apa.org

The American Psychological Association is the nation's largest scientific and professional organization representing psychology and the world's largest association of psychologists. The APA's membership includes more than 102,000 researchers, educators, clinicians, consultants, and students.

In 1993, the APA's Commission on Violence and Youth stated: "There is absolutely no doubt that higher levels of viewing violence on television are correlated with increased acceptance of aggressive attitudes and increased aggressive behavior. Three major national studies . . . reviewed hundreds of studies to arrive at the irrefutable conclusion that viewing violence increases violence. In addition, prolonged viewing of media violence can lead to emotional desensitization toward violence. . . . We call upon the Federal Communications Commission (FCC) to review, as a condition for license renewal, the programming and outreach efforts and accomplishments of television stations in helping to solve the problem of youth violence. This recommendation is consistent with the research evidence indicating television's potential to broadcast stations to 'serve the educational and informational needs of children,' both in programming and in outreach activities designed to enhance the educational value of programming. We also call on the FCC to institute rules that would require broadcasters, cable operators and other telecasters to avoid programs containing an excessive amount of dramatized violence during 'child viewing hours' between 6 A.M. and 10 P.M."

The American Academy of Pediatrics (AAP)
141 Northwest Point Blvd.
Elk Grove Village, IL 60009-0927
847-981-7873
www.apa.org

In 1997 the American Academy of Pediatrics presented the following statement to the U.S. Senate:

"The American Academy of Pediatrics, an organization of 53,000 pediatricians, offers this statement on behalf of the children and adolescents of this country. The level of violence to which they are exposed through the media has reached such horrific proportions, health professionals, parents, legislators and educators agree that something has to be done. The problem of violence on television may not appear as compelling or as urgent as immunizations, the risk of AIDS for adolescents or the need for health insurance for all children. However, in terms of overall childhood morbidity and mortality, it breeds so many problems in our society that child health experts are very concerned. Although no one holds television responsible as the sole instigator of violence, the influence of television is a factor.

"The American Academy of Pediatrics states without hesitation that televised violence has a clear and reproducible effect on the behavior of children. Televised violence contributes to the unwholesome social environment in which we live, the frequency with which violence is used to resolve conflict, and the passivity with which violence is perceived. Both epidemiological and experimental studies have demonstrated a clear relationship in children between the viewing of televised violence and violent or aggressive behavior."

The National Association for the Education of Young Children
    (NAEYC)
1509 16th St. NW
Washington, DC 20036-1426
202-232-8777 or 800-424-2460
www.naeyc.org

In 1996, the National Association for the Education of Young Children, an organization of over one hundred thousand early childhood educators, issued a position statement, "Violence in the Lives of Children," which, in part, states:

"The culture of violence is mirrored in and influenced by the media. As a result of the deregulation of the broadcasting industry, children's television and related toys have become more violent. Research is clear that the media, particularly television and films, contribute to the problem of violence in America. Research demonstrates that children who are frequent viewers of violence on television are less likely to show empathy toward the pain and suffering of others and more likely to behave aggressively."

The statement went on to call for early childhood educators ". . . to generate a sense of public outrage that motivates actions that will eliminate violence in the lives of children, families, and communities, along with restricting the marketing of violence through linkup of media, toys, and licensed products."

American Academy of Child and Adolescent Psychiatry
    (AACAP)
3615 Wisconsin Ave. NW
Washington, DC 20016
202-966-7300
www.aacap.org

This national organization, representing 6,900 psychiatrists who specialize in working with children and adolescents, produces policies and research reports on media violence. Their Media Committee periodically publishes reviews of children's films. Below is an excerpt from one of the "Facts for Families" taken from their Web site.

"American children watch an average of three to four hours of television daily. Television can be a powerful influence in developing valuing systems and shaping behavior. Ultimately, much of today's television programming is violent. Hundreds of studies of the effects of TV violence on children and teenagers have found that children may: (1) become 'immune' to the horror of violence; (2) gradually accept violence as a way to solve problems; (3) imitate the violence they observe on television; and (4) identify with certain characters, victims and/or victimizers.

"Extensive viewing of television violence by children causes greater aggressiveness. Sometimes, watching a single violent program can increase aggressiveness. Children who view shows in which violence is very realistic, frequently repeated or unpunished, are more likely to imitate what they see. Children with emotional, behavioral, learning or impulse control problems may be more easily influenced by TV violence. The impact of TV violence may be immediately evident in the child's behavior or may surface years later, and young people can even be affected when the family atmosphere shows no tendency toward violence."

The National Parent/Teacher Association (National PTA)
330 North Wabash Ave., Suite 2100
Chicago, IL 60611
800-307-4782
FAX: 312-670-6783
www.pta.org

The National Parent/Teacher Association, representing 6.5 million members, plays a pivotal role in informing and educating us about media violence. Visiting their Web site, parents can find a wealth of helpful information, including information on the rating systems, practical ideas for critical viewing, and activity sheets for dealing with media violence. The National PTA has consistently issued strong statements against TV violence, video game violence, and video game sites.

In 1993, the Convention Resolutions Committee reviewed their resolution "Violence in TV Programming," adopted in 1975. It stands in effect today.

STATEMENT ON VIOLENCE IN TV PROGRAMMING

"Whereas, children spend countless unsupervised hours watching TV; and whereas, the choice of program offerings often is less desirable, with much emphasis on violence; and whereas, children are known to imitate observed behavior and actions; and whereas, statistics reveal an alarming increase in crime committed by younger and younger children; and whereas, the Surgeon General's report states that there can be a cause-and-effect relationship between watching violence on TV and aggressive behaviors in children and young people; and whereas, at this time TV programming is self-regulated by the broadcasting industry through the National Association of Broadcasters (NAB) TV Code, a *voluntary* code not subscribed to by all stations and the provisions of which are repeatedly violated; be it therefore resolved, that the National PTA urge its state congresses, districts, councils and local units to observe and monitor TV programming and commercials in their areas; and where an excessive amount of violence in programming is seen to make known their views with documented reporting to sponsors of the program, with copies to the local TV stations, to the TV networks, to the NAB, to the Federal Communications Commission, and to their elected representatives; and be it further resolved, that the National PTA *demand* from the networks and local stations reduction in the amount of violence shown on television programs and commercials during the entire day, with particular attention to viewing hours between 2:00 P.M. and

10:00 P.M. and weekend morning hours, when impressionable children and young people are most likely to be watching; and be it further resolved, that the National PTA through its state congresses, districts, councils, and local units *demand*, if the self-regulation of programming and commercials by the broadcasting industry does not result in better TV programming with less emphasis on violence, that the Federal Communications Commission establish and enforce regulations limiting the number and percentage of programs of violence to be presented each day."

STATEMENT ON VIOLENCE IN VIDEO GAMES AND OTHER INTERACTIVE MEDIA (ADOPTED BY THE 1994 CONVENTION DELEGATES)

"Whereas, the term 'video games' is defined broadly to include any interactive computer game including all software and hardware and future developments in video game technology and interactive media; and whereas, research studies have found that, at least in the short term, children who play violent video games are significantly more aggressive afterwards than those who play less violent video games; and whereas, studies show that violent TV programs and video games have similar effects in raising children's subsequent levels of aggression; and whereas, research shows violent video games can suppress children's inclination towards engaging in pro-social behaviors; therefore be it resolved, that the National PTA, through its constituent bodies, work to educate and to increase awareness of the impact of violent video games and other interactive media; and be it further resolved, that the National PTA, through its constituent bodies, support federal legislation to provide for the development of ratings or other appropriate information systems by a commission independent of the industry to inform parents and consumers about the content of video games and other interactive media;

and be it further resolved, that the National PTA and its constituent bodies actively support efforts to end the violence in video games and other interactive media that desensitize consumers to the value of life, human or animal."

STATEMENT ON VIDEO GAME SITES
(ADOPTED BY THE 1982 BOARD OF DIRECTORS; LAST REVIEW, 1998 BY THE CONVENTION RESOLUTIONS COMMITTEE)

"National PTA is concerned about video game sites which may have an adverse effect on many of the young people who frequent such establishments. Initial studies have shown that game sites are often in close proximity to schools.

"In many cases there is not adequate control of access by school-age children during school hours, which compounds the problems of school absenteeism and truancy.

"Where little or no supervision exists, drug selling, drug use, drinking, gambling, increased gang activities, and other such behavior may be seen. Where there is diligent supervision and adequate lighting, however, the interest of the customers centers on the games and the quality of play seems to be the major concern of the youthful participants.

"State PTAs should encourage their units, councils and districts to become aware of and to educate their membership and the community regarding activities of young people at business establishment having video game machines and the impact these activities have on school attendance, alcohol and drug activity.

"PTAs should study the impact of video game arcades and other establishments where games are located. They should also work for the best possible solution that allows for reasonable use by children and youth, and at the same time does not encroach on the right of merchants to conduct their businesses."

A CHRONOLOGY OF MAJOR FINDINGS, STATEMENTS, AND ACTIONS ON MEDIA VIOLENCE, 1952–1999

Television and entertainment violence and its effects on children has been an issue since the middle of the century, although you'd barely know it. It seems that every time it captures the national consciousness, usually due to some horrendous act of schoolyard violence or a skyrocketing youth aggravated assault rate, it is presented as if it's never been discussed before. Herewith, a chronology of major findings, statements, and actions regarding media violence from 1952 to the present day. Much, if not all, of this regards television, as opposed to film and video games. Collectively, this places our fight in context, for without understanding the history of this issue, we will forever be starting over when confronting it.

1952: The U.S. House of Representatives conducts the first House committee hearings on TV violence and its impact on children. These are the first of many hearings to occur over the following decades.

1954: The U.S. Senate conducts the first Senate committee hearings on the role of television in juvenile crime.

1961: Federal Communications Commission chairman Newton N. Minow tells the National Association of Broadcasters that American TV is a "vast wasteland."

1969: The National Commission on the Causes and Prevention of Violence cites TV violence as a contributor to violence in our society.

1972: The surgeon general's office issues a report citing a link between TV/movie violence and aggressive behavior.

1975: The National Parent/Teacher Association adopts a resolution demanding that networks and local TV stations reduce the amount of violence in programs and commercials.

1976: The House of Delegates of the American Medical Association adopts a resolution "to actively oppose TV programs containing violence, as well as products and/or services sponsoring such programs," in "recognition of the fact that TV violence is a risk factor threatening the health and welfare of young Americans, indeed our future society."

1979: Parents of a fifteen-year-old convicted of murdering a neighbor initiate the first known lawsuit against TV networks (*Zamora v. CBS, et al.*), for inciting their son to violence. The suit is unsuccessful.

1982: The National Institute of Mental Health issues an extensive report stating that there is a clear consensus on the strong link between TV violence and aggressive behavior.

1984: The attorney general's Task Force on Family Violence states that evidence is overwhelming that TV violence contributes to real violence.

Leonard Eron and L. Rowell Huesmann, in a twenty-two-year study that tracked 875 boys and girls from ages eight to thirty, find that those who watched more violent television as children are more likely as adults to commit serious crimes and to use violence to punish their own children.

The American Academy of Pediatrics' Task Force on Children and Television cautions physicians and parents that TV violence promotes aggression.

1985: The American Psychological Association's Commission on Youth and Violence cites research showing a link between TV violence and real violence.

1987: Canadian broadcasters institute a voluntary code on TV violence that discourages broadcasting violent programming early in the evening.

1989: The National PTA again calls for the TV industry to reduce the amount of violence in programs.

1990: The Television Violence Act (TVA) gives three major networks (ABC, CBS, and NBC) an antitrust exemption so they can formulate a joint policy on violence.

1991: Former FCC chairman Newton Minow declares: "In 1961 I worried that my children would not benefit much from television, but in 1991 I worry that my children will actually be harmed by it."

1992: The *Journal of the American Medical Association* publishes Dr. Brandon Centerwall's study concluding that "the introduction of television into the United States in the 1950s caused a subsequent doubling of the homicide rate," and "if, hypothetically, television technology had never been developed, there would today be 10,000 fewer murders each year in the United States, 70,000 fewer rapes, and 700,000 fewer injurious assaults."

The American Psychological Association report "Big World, Small Screen" concludes that the forty years of research on the link between TV violence and real-life violence has been ignored. It goes on to state that the "scientific debate is over," and calls for federal policy to protect society.

Days before the House of Representatives hearings on TV violence, and having been forced to do so by the 1990 Television Violence Act, the broadcast industry releases a set of "voluntary" industry guidelines (called "principles") on violence.

1993: In June, major TV networks announce their agreement to air parental advisories when shows deemed violent are aired.

The National Council for Families and Television holds the industrywide Leadership Conference on Violence in Television Programming.

The Departments of Justice, Education, and Health and Human Services sponsor a major conference, calling for TV networks to consider the social effects of media violence when designing programming.

1994: The Center for Media and Public Affairs conducts a study of television violence and finds that from 1992 to 1994, depictions of serious violence on television increased 67 percent.

1998: The National Television Violence Study concludes that 60 percent of all TV programs are violent and that "there are substantial risks of harmful effects from viewing violence throughout the television environment."

The publication of "Children and Media Violence: A Yearbook from the UNESCO International Clearinghouse on Children and Violence on the Screen." It reviews worldwide studies of media violence from twenty-five countries and outlines the world's concern about the "global aggressive culture" being formed by violent television, particularly violent U.S. television and film.

1999: President Clinton initiates a study by the FTA and the Attorney General of the strategies of marketing violent media to children.

WHERE TO VOICE YOUR CONCERNS

As its subtitle says, this book is a call to action. Here's where to call, write, fax, E-mail, and visit for action on this issue. We suggest contacting the following television broadcast and cable networks, major movie studios, theaters, pertinent organizations, government offices, and toy companies to voice your concerns about violent entertainment. But we also encourage you to let those people and organizations know when they're helping to make a positive difference.

TELEVISION STATIONS

(Note: The Telecommunications Act of 1996 requires television stations to make available a staff person to act as a liaison with viewers who want to comment on children's programs.)

ABC
Audience Information Dept.
77th West 66th St., 9th Floor
New York, NY 10023
212-456-7477

ABC Entertainment
2040 Avenue of the Stars
Los Angeles, CA 90067
310-557-5413 or 800-213-6222

A&E/Arts and Entertainment
235 East 45th St.
New York, NY 10017
212-210-1340

AMC/American Movie Classics
1111 Stewart Ave.
Bethpage, NY 11714
516-364-2222

CBS
Audience Services
530 West 57th St.
New York, NY 10019
212-975-3247

CNN
One CNN Center
Atlanta, GA 30348-5366
404-827-1500

COM/Comedy Central
Attention: Dennay Riley
1775 Broadway
New York, NY 10019
212-767-8600

Discovery Channel
7700 Wisconsin Ave., Suite 700
Bethesda, MD 20814
301-986-0444

Disney Channel
3800 West Alameda Ave.
Burbank, CA 91505
800-822-8648
FAX: 818-842-1024

ESPN
935 Middle St.
Bristol, CT 06010
860-585-2236

FOX Broadcast Studios
PO Box 900
Beverly Hills, CA 90213
310-369-1000

HBO/Home Box Office
1100 Avenue of the Americas
New York, NY 10036
212-512-1000

Lifetime
Viewer Services
309 West 49th St.
New York, NY 10019
212-424-7000

MTV (owns VH-1 and Nickelodeon)
Viewer Comments
1515 Broadway, 24th Floor
New York, NY 10036
212-258-8000

NBC
30 Rockefeller Plaza
New York, NY 10112
212-664-2333

NICK/Nickelodeon
1515 Broadway, 42nd Floor
New York, NY 10036
212-258-7500

PBS
Attention: Program Information
1320 Braddock Pl.
Alexandria, VA 22314
703-739-5000

SHO/Showtime
1633 Broadway
New York, NY 10019
212-708-1600

TNN (The Nashville Network)
2806 Opryland Drive
Nashville, TN 37214
615-883-7000

TNT/Turner Network TV
1050 Techwood Drive NW
Atlanta, GA 30318
404-885-4538

USA Network
Viewer Response

1230 Avenue of the Americas
New York, NY 10020
212-408-9100

VH-1/Contemporary Music Videos
1515 Broadway
New York, NY 10036
212-258-7800

MAJOR STUDIOS: MOTION PICTURES, HOME VIDEOS, TV MOVIES

Columbia Pictures Entertainment Company, or
Sony Pictures Entertainment, Inc., or
Tri-Star Pictures
10202 West Washington Blvd.
Culver City, CA 90232
310-244-4000

MGM Communications Co.
Attention: William Mitchell
2500 Broadway St.
Santa Monica, CA 90404-3061
310-449-3000

Paramount Communications, Inc.
Publicity Department
1515 Broadway
New York, NY 10036
212-846-4320

Paramount Pictures and Home Videos
Bluhdorn Building

5555 Melrose Ave.
Hollywood, CA 90038-3917
323-956-5000

The Samuel Goldwyn Company
10203 Santa Monica Blvd.
Los Angeles, CA 90067-6403
310-552-2255

The Samuel Goldwyn Company
Attention: Publicity Department
1133 Broadway
New York, NY 10010
212-367-9435

Twentieth Century-Fox Film Corporation
10201 West Pico Blvd.
Los Angeles, CA 90035
310-369-1000

Universal Pictures
100 Universal City Plaza
Universal City, CA 91608
818-777-1000

The Walt Disney Company
500 South Buena Vista St.
Burbank, CA 91521
818-560-1581

Warner Brothers, Inc. (a division of Time Warner, Inc.)
4000 Warner Blvd.
Burbank, CA 91522
818-954-6000

THEATERS
Cineplex Odeon Corporation
1303 Yonge St.
Toronto, Ontario
Canada M4T 2Y9
416-323-6600

General Cinema Corporation
Director of Operations
1280 Boylston St.
Chestnut Hill, MA 02467
800-992-0084

For comments on the film rating system:

Motion Picture Association of America, Inc.
Jack Valenti, President
1600 Eye St. NW
Washington, DC 20006
202-293-1966

For comments on the video and computer game rating system:

Entertainment Software Rating Board (ESRB)
845 3rd Ave.
New York, NY 10022
800-771-3772
www.ersb.org

VIDEO RENTAL COMPANIES
Blockbuster Videos
Corporate Office

1201 Elm St.
Dallas, TX 75270
214-854-3000

Tower Records/Video
Customer Comments/Video Rental
MTS, Inc.
2500 Del Monte St., Building C
West Sacramento, CA 95691-9001
916-373-2500 or 800-541-0070

VIDEO AND COMPUTER GAMES
Nintendo of America, Inc.
Corporate Communication Manager
4820 150th Ave. NE
Redmond, WA 98052
425-882-2040
FAX: 425-882-3585

Sega of America
650 Townsend St., Suite 650
San Francisco, CA 94065
415-701-6000

To voice your opinion about a coin-operated video game
parental advisory system, contact:

American Amusement Machine Association (AAMA)
450 East Higgins Rd., Suite 201
Elk Grove Village, IL 60007
847-290-9088
www.coin-op.org

The AAMA is a nonprofit trade association that represents approximately 120 manufacturers, distributors, and parts suppliers of coin-operated amusement equipment.

International Association of Family Entertainment Centers
(IAFEC)
36 Symonds Rd.
Hillsborough, NH 03244
603-464-6498
E-mail: IAFECnh@aol.com

GOVERNMENT OFFICIALS
Federal Communications Commission
Mass Media Bureau
Complaints/Enforcement Division
Political Programming Branch, Room 3443
445 12th St. SW
Washington, DC 20554
202-418-1430

The President of the United States
The White House
1600 Pennsylvania Ave.
Washington, DC
202-456-1414

TOY MANUFACTURERS AND RETAILERS
Lewis Galoob Toys
500 Forbes Blvd.
San Francisco, CA 94080
650-952-1678

Hasbro Toy Group
1027 Newport Ave.
Pawtucket, RI 02862
401-431-8697

Mattel Toys
333 Continental Blvd.
El Segundo, CA 90245
310-252-2000

Saban Entertainment
400 West Alameda Ave.
Burbank, CA 91505
818-972-4800

Toys R Us Corporate Office
CEO Robert Nakasone
461 From Rd.
Paramus, NJ 07652
210-262-7800

MEDIA LITERACY AND
VIOLENCE PREVENTION
ORGANIZATIONS

We're not alone out there. There are several worthwhile watch-dog groups that have been fighting the good fight for years. The following is a list of media literacy and violence prevention organizations, along with their statements of purpose.

Americans for Responsible Television
(The Dove Foundation)
4521 Broadmoor SE
Grand Rapids, MI 49512
616-514-5000 or 800-968-8437
www.dove.org

Established to encourage and promote the creation, production, and distribution of wholesome family entertainment, the Dove Foundation, free from commercial pressures, awards a blue-and-white Dove Seal to any movie or video that is rated "family friendly" by its film review board.

Atrium Society Publications
PO Box 816
Middlebury, VT 05753
800-848-6021
www.atriumsoc.org

The Atrium Society offers understanding about the conditioned mind, "which has brought us to a state of unparalleled conflict and devastation that we experience in the world today." Its intent is to bring the issue of conditioning, and the tremendous conflict conditioning creates, to the forefront of awareness and consideration. Resources include a series of books for youth on understanding and handling violence; books for parents, such as *Growing Up Sane: Understanding the Conditioned Mind*; audio/videotapes; teacher training workshops; and seminars to address the primary causes of conflict.

Canadians Concerned About Violence in Entertainment
    (C-CAVE)
416-961-0853
FAX: 416-929-2720
E-mail: rdyson@oise.utoronto.ca

Founded in 1983 in collaboration with the U.S.-based National Coalition on Television Violence, Canadians Concerned About Violence in Entertainment provides public education on the results of media violence research and believes the public has a right to know that the overwhelming weight of research points toward harmful effects. The organization functions primarily as a working group through media interviews and the provision of information to journalists and other members of the media. C-CAVE maintains links with a broad coalition of groups, both nationally and internationally.

Center for Media Literacy
4727 Wilshire Blvd., Suite 403
Los Angeles, CA 90010
800-226-9494
FAX: 323-931-4474
www.medialit.org

The Center for Media Literacy distributes a broad range of media literacy education books, kits, and videos for parents and teachers, including the highly acclaimed *Beyond Blame: Challenging Violence in the Media*. This kit applies the principles of media literacy education to violence reduction and prevention. It contains lesson plans, ready-to-use handouts, and audio/video resources for all age groups. A comprehensive catalog of all resources offered is available.

Center for the Study and Prevention of Violence
Institute for Behavorial Sciences
University of Colorado, Boulder
Campus Box 442
Boulder, CO 80309-0442
303-492-8147

The Center for the Study and Prevention of Violence provides guidance on research, effective programs, and policy actions that improve the effectiveness of antiviolence interventions. Among the reports available is *What Works in Reducing Adolescent Violence: An Empirical Review of the Field* by Patrick Tolan and Nancy Guerra.

Center for Successful Parenting
1917 East 116th Street
Carmel, IN 46032
317-581-5355
Fax: 317-581-5399
E-mail: sstoughton@stoughtongroup.com.

Founded in 1997, the Center for Successful Parenting is presently focused on media violence because the founders believe that protecting children from the negative impact of media violence is key for adults of the next generation to be mentally and socially healthy. The group is organizing the ever-growing body of research demonstrating the negative effects of media violence, along with a national parent awareness campaign.

Committee for Children
2203 Airport Way S., Suite 500
Seattle, WA 98134
800-634-4449

The Committee for Children is an international nonprofit organization whose mission is to promote the safety, well-being, and social development of children by creating quality educational programs for educators, families, and communities. The pre-kindergarten–to–grade 9 violence prevention curriculum, *Second Step,* teaches children prosocial skills and includes a companion program for parent education at the elementary level. *Second Step* implementation has taken place in approximately ten thousand schools across North America. A study published in the *Journal of the American Medical Association* (May 27, 1997) demonstrates *Second Step*'s effectiveness in changing children's behavior.

Cultural Environment Movement (CEM)
PO Box 40285
Philadelphia, PA 19106
E-mail: CEM@libertynet.org

The Cultural Environment Movement is a nonprofit coalition of independent organizations and individual supporters in every state of the United States and in fifty-seven other countries on six continents, united in working for freedom, fairness, gender equity, general diversity, and democratic decision-making in media ownership, employment, and representation. The organization supports, and if necessary organizes, local and national media councils, study groups, citizen groups, minority and professional groups, and other forums of public discussion, policy development, representation, and action. Not waiting for a blueprint, it creates and experiments with methods of community and citizen participation in local, national, and international media policy-making.

The Fathers' Network
PO Box 800-SH
San Anselmo, CA 94979
415-453-2839
www.menstuff.org

The goal of this organization is to increase fathers' involvement in parenting and to promote fulfilling relationships between fathers and children. Much useful information can be found on their Web site for men who want to make a difference in a child's life.

GrowSmartBrains
PO Box 311
Redmond, WA 98073-0311
206-654-2994
www.GrowSmartBrains.com

Author Gloria DeGaetano and her staff of highly trained educators and consultants offer research-based, application-rich workshops across the United States and Canada for corporations, school districts, social service, and parent organizations. Emphasis is on the impact of screen technologies on brain development and the problematic effects of violent entertainment on children's learning and behavior. GrowSmartBrains provides manuals (in English and Spanish) and educational audio- and videotapes, including *Maximizing Your Child's Potential: Healthy Brain Development in a Media Age*, a forty-minute video for parents of young children.

Heavy Freight Films
811 First Avenue, Suite 425
Seattle, WA 98104
Contacts:
Richard Hazzard, M.Ed.
206-755-3118
FAX: 206-621-1193
Sandy Cioffi
206-322-1332
FAX: 206-322-1341

Two of Washington State's leading media literacy specialists founded Heavy Freight Films with the intention of creating unique opportunities for individual and social change through media education, addressing issues such as violence prevention, youth leadership, and community involvement. Their projects include consulting with school districts for adopting media literacy standards, extensive teacher training programs, conducting innovative film schools for youth, and community film projects with professional filmmakers mentoring youth in film production. One video production, *Terminal 187,* produced by and for youth, is an excellent, compelling examination of the consequences of violence for anyone who cares about kids.

Institute on Violence and Destructive Behavior
1265 University of Oregon
Eugene, OR 97403-1265

541-346-3591
http://interact.uoregon.edu/ivdb/ivdb.html

The Institute on Violence and Destructive Behavior is doing some of the most seminal research in the area of violence prevention today. Its mission is to empower schools and social service agencies to address violence and destructive behavior, at the point of school entry and beyond, in order to ensure safety and to facilitate the academic achievement and healthy social development of children and youth. Key target areas addressed are antisocial behavior, school failure, delinquency, violence, gang membership, and at-risk conditions. Call for a list of publications and research studies currently available.

Lion and the Lamb Project
4300 Montgomery Ave., Suite 104
Bethesda, MD 20814
301-654-3091
FAX: 301-718-8192
www.lionlamb.org

The Lion and the Lamb Project provides information about the effects of violent entertainment, toys, and games on children's behavior for parents, teachers, day-care providers, social workers, psychologists, grandparents, and others—anyone interested in teaching values of nonviolence to children. They offer four different types of workshops, along with a Parent Action Kit, which provides suggestions for selecting age-appropriate, nonviolent toys and games, and tips for resolving family conflicts peacefully at home and on the playground.

Media Awareness Network
1500 Merivale Rd., 3rd Floor

Nepean, ON
Canada K2E 6Z5
613-224-7721
FAX: 613-224-1958
E-mail: info@media-awareness.ca
www.media-awareness.ca

The Media Awareness Network (MNet) is a nonprofit organization promoting media education among children and young people. MNet's award-winning Web site is one of the largest educational Web sites in Canada. It provides parents, educators, and community leaders with free, copyright-cleared on-line resources and information on a variety of issues related to children and the media, including media violence, advertising to children, and children and the Internet.

Media Education Foundation
26 Center St.
Northampton, MA 01060
413-584-8500
E-mail: mediaed@mediaed.org
www.igc.org/mef
video orders: 800-897-0080

Directed by well-known media scholar and author Sut Jhally, this foundation produces and distributes award-wining resources for students of media literacy, educators, parents, and community leaders. *The Killing Screens: Media and the Culture of Violence* is an educational video that examines the psychology, sociology, and politics of media violence. In the video, paced for high school and college students, Dr. George Gerbner addresses the issue of living and growing within a cultural environment of pervasive violent representation. Social critic Neil Postman says of this video: "If every American could see *The Killing Screens* there would ensue a revolution in the content of popular media. "

Mediascope, Inc.
12711 Ventura Blvd., Suite 440
Studio City, CA 91604
818-508-2080
www.mediascope.org

Mediascope is a national, nonprofit research and public policy organization working to raise awareness about the influence of media on society. Founded in 1992, the organization works with the entertainment industry to encourage responsible depictions of health and social issues, particularly as they relate to children and adolescents. They address such topics as media violence, ratings, teen sexuality, effects of video games, artists' rights and responsibilities, and substance abuse. Mediascope's resources and services are used by screenwriters, journalists, researchers, producers, media critics, educators, lawyers, media executives, legislators, government officials, advocacy groups, and students.

MediaWise
PO Box 6145
Kansas City, KS 66106
913-831-3221
FAX: 913-831-0262

MediaWise operates through a broad-based coalition of community groups to reduce the impact and incidence of violence in the media through public awareness, education, and community action without invading First Amendment rights. They provide programs and services to help children, youth, and adults become discriminating media consumers by learning how to analyze, evaluate, and interpret the messages and images delivered by the various forms of media in our society. They offer *MediaSmarts,* an innovative video-based media literacy and antiviolence curriculum for use in middle schools or by youth-serving agencies.

Mothers Against Violence in America (MAVIA)
105-14th Ave., Suite 2A
Seattle, WA 98122
206-323-2303
800-897-7697
FAX: 206-323-2132
www.mavia.org

Mothers Against Violence in America is a national, nonprofit, nonpartisan educational organization dedicated to reducing violence by and against children. Founded in 1994, with over thirty-five thousand members, MAVIA encourages prevention investment in young people before they are affected by violence, and advocates for changes that support a safer environment. MAVIA's innovative programs, such as Students Against Violence Everywhere (SAVE) and violent video game legislative initiatives, have been praised by President and Mrs. Clinton as exemplary models of grassroots activism.

National Alliance for Non-Violent Programming (NANP)
122 North Elm St., Suite 300
Greensboro, NC 27401
336-370-0392
FAX: 336-370-0407
E-mail: NA4NVP@aol.com

A network of national not-for-profit organizations including the American Medical Women's Association, Jack and Jill of America,

Jewish Women International, the National Association of Women Business Owners, National Council of LaRaza, and Soroptimist of the Americas, the National Alliance for Non-Violent Programming's reach into communities extends to over two million citizens at the grassroots level. NANP researches and recommends noncensorial resources, workshops, and educational materials appropriate for children and youth, parents, teachers, caregivers, service organizations, violence prevention efforts, and the faith community. Once a community initiative is launched, NANP provides technical assistance and support to ensure sustainability.

National Coalition on Television Violence (NCTV)
51332 Newport Ave.
Bethesda, MD 20816
E-mail: nctvmd@aol.com
www.nctvv.org

Since 1980 the National Coalition on Television Violence has been providing useful information regarding the amount of TV violence, the accuracy of rating systems, and practical tips for citizen advocacy. Directed by MaryAnn Banta, the organization responds to E-mail and acts as a clearinghouse to direct inquires to the most helpful resources available nationwide.

National Institute on Media and the Family
606 24th Ave. S., Suite 606
Minneapolis, MN 55454
888-672-5437
FAX: 612-672-4113
www.mediafamily.org

The National Institute on Media and the Family is a nonprofit organization whose mission is to maximize the benefits and minimize the harm of media on children and families through research, education, and advocacy. The organization provides a range of educational resources for parents, teachers, and community leaders, including a comprehensive alternative rating system for violent media and MediaWise, a multimedia resource kit that provides innovative, action-oriented solutions to the question "What can we do about the powerful influence of media on our children's lives?" Visit their Web site for current lists of the most violent and dangerous as well as the best video and computer games for our kids.

Teachers Resisting Unhealthy Children's Entertainment (TRUCE)
PO Box 441261
Somerville, MA 02144

Teachers Resisting Unhealthy Children's Entertainment is a national group of educators deeply concerned about how children's entertainment and toys are affecting the play and behavior of children in the classroom. TRUCE publishes a valuable newsletter and works to raise public awareness about the negative effects of violent and stereotyped toys and media on children, families, schools, and society.

Turn Off the TV
800-949-8688
www.turnoffthetv.com

The mission of Turn Off the TV is to bring people together by encouraging families and friends to turn off the television and spend time playing, learning, and communicating. A catalog of resources is available by calling the above toll-free number. By visiting their Web site, parents will find loads of fun ideas for children in all stages of development who say, "I'm bored; there's nothing to do."

NOTES

INTRODUCTION

Adolescents who copy crimes . . . correct flaws that may have caused the television crime to fail: Wendy Josephson, "Television Violence: A Review of the Effects on Children of Different Ages." Ottawa: National Clearinghouse on Family Violence, 1995, 40.

Scientific evidence has established that screen portrayals of violence need not lead to reinforcement of aggressive attitudes and behaviors . . . Joel Federman, *Television Violence Study*, vol. 3. Santa Barbara: University of California, 1998, 7–11.

CHAPTER 1: IT'S A VIOLENT WORLD AFTER ALL

According to InterPol, between 1977 and 1993 the per capita "serious assault" rate increased . . . InterPol International Crime Statistics, InterPol, Lyons, France, vols. 1977 to 1994.

The Japanese crime data (30 percent increase in juvenile violent crime in 1997): BBC News Online, "Japanese tackle teenage knife attacks," Friday, February 6, 1998.

According to FBI reports, crime is down 7 percent: Fox Butterfield, "Crime Fell 7 Percent in '98, Continuing a 7-Year Trend," *The New York Times*, May 17, 1999, 14.

From 1960 through 1991 the U.S. population increased by 40 percent, yet violent crime increased by 500 percent; murders increased by 170 percent, rapes 520 percent, and aggravated assaults 600 percent: Ronald Kotulak, *Inside the Brain: Revolutionary Discoveries of How the Mind Works.* Kansas City: Andrews McMeel Publishing, 1996, 69.

In 1996 there were 19,654 murders, 95,769 reported rapes, over 1 million cases of aggravated assault, and 537,050 robberies, amounting to a loss of about $500 million in stolen property: Federal Bureau of Investigation, *Crime in the United States 1996, Uniform Crime Reporting Statistics.* Washington, D.C.; U.S. Department of Justice, 1996.

Murder is the least committed violent crime, although the most often reported crime on the nightly news: Howard Kurtz of *The Washington Post,* "Murder Rates Fall—But Not on Network News," *The Seattle Times,* August 13, 1997, A9.

Figure 1—Violent Crime in America: "Statistical Abstract of the United States." Washington, D.C.: The U.S. Department of Commerce, Bureau of the Census, editions 1957 to 1997.

Professor James Q. Wilson quote: Lt. Col. Dave Grossman, *On Killing: The Psychological Cost of Learning to Kill in War and Society.* New York: Little, Brown & Co., 1996, 301.

According to the U.S. Army Medical Service Corps, a hypothetical wound that . . . Dave Grossman, "Evolution of Weaponry," in *Encyclopedia of Violence: Peace and Conflict.* New York: Academic Press, 1999.

The per capita incarceration rate in America more than quadrupled between 1970, when it was at 97 people per 100,000, and 1997, when it reached 440 per 100,000: Statistical Abstract of the United States. Washington, D.C.: The U.S. Department of Commerce, Bureau of the Census, editions 1957 to 1997.

John J. DiIulio quote: Lt. Col. Dave Grossman, *On Killing: The Psychological Cost of Learning to Kill in War and Society.* New York: Little, Brown & Co., 1996, 301.

In Richmond . . . "zero tolerance" . . . has been credited with cutting murders by 65 percent: Virginia Governor James Gilmore, quoted in Virginia Governor James Gilmore, quoted in *U.S. News & World Report,* November 16, 1998.

In Boston . . . led to an 80 percent drop in youth homicides from 1990 to 1995, and in 1996 not a single youth died in a firearm homicide: President Clinton, *State of the Union Address,* "The President's Anti-Gang and Youth Violence Strategy—An Overview," February 4, 1997.

Among young people fifteen to twenty-four years old, murder is the second-leading cause of death. For African-American youths, murder is number one; Every 5 minutes a child is arrested in America for committing a violent crime, and gun-related violence takes the life of an American child every three hours; A child growing up in Washington, D.C., or Chicago is fifteen times more likely to be murdered than a child in Northern Ireland: Ellen Wartella, Adriana Olivarez, Nancy Jennings, "Children and Television Violence in the United States," in *Children and Media Violence: Yearbook from the UNESCO International Clearinghouse on Children and Violence on the Screen,* eds. U. Carlsson and C. Von Felitzen. Nordicom: Goteborg University, 1998, 55.

. . . 4,881 gangs in the United States: Daniel Flannery, C. Ronald Huff, Michael Manos, "Youth Gangs: A Developmental Perspective," in *Delinquent Violent Youth: Theory and Interventions,* eds. T. Gullotta, G. Adams, R. Montemayor. Thousand Oaks: Sage Publications, 1998, 176.

Since 1960 teen suicide has tripled: John Crudele and Richard Erickson, *Making Sense of Adolescence: How to Parent from the Heart.* Minneapolis: John Crudele Productions, 1995, 139.

Every day an estimated 270,000 students bring guns to school; One of every fifty children has a parent in prison: Ronald Kotulak, *Inside the Brain: Revolutionary Discoveries of How the Mind Works.* Kansas City: Andrews McMeel Publishing, 1997, 93.

At least 160,000 children miss school every day because they fear an attack or intimidation by other students: National Education Association statistics, in Suellen Fried and Paula Fried, *Bullies and Victims: Helping Your Child Through the Schoolyard Battlefield.* New York: M. Evans and Company, 1996, xii.

One out of three girls and one out of seven boys are sexually abused by the time they reach the age of eighteen: Ellen Bass and Laura Davis, *The Courage to Heal—A Guide for Women Survivors of Child Sexual Abuse.* New York: Harper & Row, Publishers, 1988, 20.

Figures 2 and 3—Violent Crime Arrest Rate for Juvenile Males and Juvenile Females: Graphs compiled by authors using data from Federal Bureau of Investigation, *Crime in the United States 1996, Uniform Crime Reporting Statistics.* Washington, D.C.: U.S. Department of Justice, 1996.

Stephen M. Case, of America Online, says that 80 percent of teenagers on AOL say that what happened at Columbine could happen in their school. Ken Auletta. "What I Did at Summer Camp," *The New Yorker,* July 26, 1999, 48.

Diane Levin quote: Ann Cornell, "TV, Video Game Violence Cause Aggressive Behavior, Leads to Crime, Experts Warn,"

Lion and Lamb Newsletter, Video Game Violence (Internet Information).

CHAPTER 2: NOT JUST A "TOASTER WITH PICTURES"

Brandon Tartikoff quote: John Caputo, "Tune Out the Tube: television viewing poor substitute for summer recreation," *The Spokesman-Review,* June 30, 1991, A-17.

Since 1950 there has been a total of more than 3,500 research studies . . . Ellen Wartella, Adriana Olivarez, Nancy Jennings, "Children and Television Violence in the United States," in *Children and Media Violence: Yearbook from the UNESCO International Clearinghouse on Children and Violence on the Screen,* eds. U. Carlsson and C. Von Felitzen. Nordicom: Goteborg University, 1998, 57.

One random analysis of almost 1,000 of these studies found that all save 18 (12 of those were funded by the television industry) demonstrate . . . Dr. Scott Snyder, in a 1998 presentation at the annual meeting of the American College of Forensic Psychiatry. "Clinical Psychiatry News," International Medical News Group, 1998, 26(7), 36.

In the myriad studies done over the last four decades, experts have found three basic negative effects . . . "Safeguarding Our Youth: Violence Prevention for Our Nation's Children, Report from the Working Group on Media." Washington, D.C., Center for Media Literacy, July 20–21, 1993, 4.

Since 1982, television violence has increased 780 percent . . . Phil Phillips, *Saturday Morning Mind Control.* Nashville: Oliver-Nelson Books, 1991, 54.

The first U.S. Congressional hearings on the question took place in 1952 . . . John P. Murray, "Studying Television Violence: A Research Agenda for the 21st Century," in *Research Par-*

adigms, Television, and Social Behavior, eds. Joy Asamen and Gordon Berry. Thousand Oaks: Sage Publications, 1998, 370.

. . . *when only around a quarter of American households had television sets* . . . Dr. Brandon Centerwall, "Journal of the American Medical Association," June 10, 1992–vol. 267, no. 22, "Television and violence: The scale of the problem and where to go from here," page 3,061, fig. 2.

. . . *the "university of the air" brought quality programming* . . . Mary Megee, *On Television: Teach the Children,* a video. San Francisco: California Newsreel, 1991.

Concerns about television violence in the mid-50s . . . totally unacceptable risk: John P. Murray, "Impact of Televised Violence," Kansas State University, www.ksu.edu/humec/impact.htm, 1–2.

In 1969, Senator John Pastore . . . invited the Surgeon General . . . John P. Murray, "Children and Television Violence," *Kansas Journal of Law and Public Policy,* vol. no. 3 (1995), 10.

1972 Surgeon General's Report: Surgeon General's Scientific Advisory Committee on Television and Social Behavior, *Television and Growing Up: The Impact of Television Violence.* Washington, D.C.: Government Printing Office, 1972.

Quote from the National Institute of Mental Health Report: Pearl D. Bouthilet, L. Lazar, J. Eds. *National Institute of Mental Health, Television and Behavior: Ten Years of Scientific Progress and Implications for the Eighties, vol. 1,* Summary Report. Washington D.C.: United States Government Printing Office, 1982.

Eron and Huesmann's study: L. D. Eron and L. R. Huesmann, "The Control of Aggressive Behavior by Changes in Attitudes, Values, and the Conditions of Learning," in *Advances in the Study of Aggression,* eds. R. J. Blanchard and D. C. Blanchard. Orlando: Academic Press, Inc., 1984, 139–171.

McBeth Williams's study: Tannis McBeth Williams, *The Impact of Television: A Natural Experiment in Three Communities.* New York: Academic Press, 1986.

Centerwall's study: Brandon Centerwall, "Television and Violence: The Scale of the Problem and Where to Go from Here," *The Journal of the American Medical Association,* vol. 267 (June 10, 1992), 3059–3063.

"There never was a moment of 'Aha!' It simply happened": Gloria DeGaetano, personal interview with Dr. Brandon Centerwall, June 15, 1998.

In a classic 1974 study . . . Ronald Drabman and Margaret Thomas, "Does media violence increase children's toleration of real-life aggression?" *Developmental Psychology,* vol. 10, 1974, 418–421.

. . . one of the more benign movies of the 1990s . . . Vincent Canby's observations in Michael Medved, *Hollywood vs. America: Popular Culture and the War on Traditional Values.* New York: HarperCollins, 1992, 187.

Miller quote: Michael Medved, *Hollywood vs. America: Popular Culture and the War on Traditional Values.* New York: HarperCollins, 1992, 190–191.

Power Rangers contains about two hundred acts of violence per hour: Chris J. Boyatzis, "Of Power Rangers and V-Chips," *Young Children,* vol. 52, no. 7 (November 1997), 75.

... cartoons averaging twenty-five acts of violence per hour: A. Huston, E. Donnerstein, et al., *Big World, Small Screen: The Role of Television in American Society.* Lincoln: University of Nebraska Press, 1992, 136.

British children under the age of twelve were not allowed to see Batman: "Batman Off Limits to Kids in Britain," Reuter Press, *Seattle Post-Intelligencer,* July 31, 1989, C-5.

Swedish children under the age of fifteen ... Turtles movies. Description of audiences for films by Swedish Bureau of Censors, www.statensbiografbyra.se.

Fright reactions: "Problems Frequently Caused by Scary Television and Movies," in Joanne Cantor, *Mommy, I'm Scared: How TV and Movies Frighten Children and What We Can Do to Protect Them.* Orlando: Harcourt Brace & Company, 1998, 215.

Cantor quote: Joanne Cantor, Ph.D., *Mommy, I'm Scared: How TV and Movies Frighten Children and What We Can Do to Protect Them.* Orlando: Harcourt Brace & Company, 1998, 12–13.

23 million Americans suffer from some sort of anxiety-based disorder: Stephen Hall, "Fear Itself: What we know about how it works, how it can be treated and what it tells us about our unconscious," *The New York Times Magazine,* February 28, 1999, 44.

Hall quote: Stephen Hall, "Fear Itself: What we know about how it works, how it can be treated and what it tells us about our unconscious," *The New York Times Magazine,* February 28, 1999, 45.

George Gerbner study: George Gerbner and Nancy Signorielli, *Violence Profile, 1967 Through 1988–89: Enduring Patterns,* manuscript. Philadelphia: University of Pennsylvania, Annenberg School of Communication, 1990; George Gerbner, et al., "Growing Up with Television: The Cultivation Perspective," in J. Bryant and D. Zillmann (eds.), *Media Effects: Advances in Theory and Research.* Hillsdale: Lawrence Erlbaum, 17–41.

Center for Media and Public Affairs study: R. Lichter and D. Amundson, "A Day of Television Violence." Washington, D.C.: Center for Media and Public Affairs, 1992; R. Lichter and D. Amundson, "A Day of TV Violence: 1992 vs. 1994." Washington, D.C.: Center for Media and Public Affairs, 1994; Elizabeth Kolbert, "Study Finds TV Violence on the Rise," *The New York Times,* August 5, 1994, A9.

Newton Minow quote: Newton Minow quoted in E. Barnouw, *Tube of Plenty: The Evolution of American Television* (New York: Oxford University Press, 1975), 300.

Mark Fowler quote: C. Mayer, "FCC Chief's Fears: Fowler Sees Threat in Regulation," *Washington Post,* February 6, 1983, K-6.

. . . in the 1980–81 season, when the FCC was discussing deregulation of children's programming, violence on children's television shows reached its highest level in twenty years: thirty-three acts of violence per hour: John P. Murray, "Impact of Televised Violence," Kansas State University, www.ksu.edu/humec/impact.htm, 5.

By 1987, the sales of violent toys had soared more than 600 percent: Levin, Diane, *Remote Control Childhood? Combating the Hazards of Media Culture.* Washington, D.C.:

National Association for the Education of Young Children, 1998, 10.

Television Violence Act: Newsletter from Senator Paul Simon, December 12, 1990.

Children's Television Act: Brian Sullivan, "Children's TV Bill Becomes Law," National Coalition on Television Violence Press Release, December 28, 1990.

. . . such programs as G.I. Joe, Leave It to Beaver, The Jetsons, *and* James Bond, Jr. . . . Newton Minow and Craig Lamay, "Making Television Safe for Kids," book excerpt in *Time,* June 26, 1995, 70; Cox News Service, "TV Stations Say 'Toons, Reruns Teach Kids," *Bellevue Journal American,* August 30, 1992, B-6.

The 1990 Report, Watching America quote: Michael Medved, *Hollywood vs. America: Popular Culture and the War on Traditional Values.* New York: HarperCollins, 1992, 196–197.

Barry Diller quote: Terry Pristin, "Soul-Searching on Violence by the Industry," *The Los Angeles Times,* May 18, 1992, Home Section, 1.

National Association of Broadcasters "Statement of Principles": Advisory Committee on Public Interest Obligations of Digital Television Broadcasters, "Statement of Principles of Radio and Television Broadcasting," Issued by the Board of Directors of the National Association of Broadcasters, adopted, 1990; reaffirmed 1992.

National Television Violence Study: George Comstock, "Television Research: Past Problems and Present Issues," in *Research Paradigms, Television, and Social Behavior,* eds.

Joy Asamen and Gordon Berry. Thousand Oaks: Sage Publications, 1998, 32.

The broadcast industry . . . financed its own three-year study: George Comstock, "Television Research: Past Problems and Present Issues," in *Research Paradigms, Television, and Social Behavior,* eds. Joy Asamen and Gordon Berry. Thousand Oaks: Sage Publications, 1998, 32.

Facts from National Television Study: Federman, Joel (ed.), *National Television Violence Study, Vol. 3, Executive Summary.* Santa Barbara: University of California, 1998, 29–42.

Marty Franks quote: Jeannine Aversa (The Associated Press), "Prime-Time Television on the Rise," *The Seattle Times,* April, 16, 1998, A-3.

George Comstock quote: George Comstock, "Television Research: Past Problems and Present Issues," in *Research Paradigms, Television, and Social Behavior,* eds. Joy Asamen and Gordon Berry. Thousand Oaks: Sage Publications, 1998, 32.

. . . the largest study ever conducted which surveyed five thousand twelve-year-olds in twenty-three countries . . . Jo Grobel, "The UNESCO Global Study on Media Violence: Report Presented to the Director General of UNESCO," in *Children and Media Violence: Yearbook from the UNESCO International Clearinghouse on Children and Violence on the Screen,* eds. U. Carlsson and C. Von Felitzen. Nordicom: Goteborg University, 1998, 181–199.

A recent study examining 2,380 major movie releases from 1988 to 1997 indicates . . . Armstrong Williams, "Extra! Extra! Family-friendly films make money for Hollywood," *Eastside Journal,* June 6, 1999, B-4.

CHAPTER 3: PRETENDING TO BE FREDDY KRUEGER

Many believe that the desire for murderous violence is largely unnatural: Lt. Col. Dave Grossman, "Psychological effects of Combat," in *The Oxford Companion to American Military History.* New York: Oxford University Press, 1999.

Brigadier General S. L. A. Marshall first observed . . . by nature, are not close-range, interpersonal killers: S. L. A. Marshall, *Men Against Fire.* Gloucester: Peter Smith, 1978, 51, 78–79.

A preschooler . . . is exposed to nearly 10,000 violent episodes each year . . . Federman, Joel (ed.), *National Television Violence Study, Vol. 3, Executive Summary.* Santa Barbara: University of California, 1998, 34.

Nearly 40 percent of all violent incidents on television are initiated by characters who possess qualities that make them attractive role models to kids . . . More than half of violent incidents feature physical aggression that would be lethal or incapacitating if it were to occur in real life: Federman, Joel (ed.), *National Television Violence Study, Vol. 3, Executive Summary.* Santa Barbara: University of California, 1998, 29.

By age eighteen, a typical American child will have seen at least two hundred thousand dramatized acts of violence and forty thousand screen murders: President Clinton, in his national address on media violence following the Littleton Massacre.

Poussaint quote: Poussaint, Alvin M.D., "Taking Movie Ratings Seriously: The Risks Faced by Children Allowed to Watch Films Meant for Adults Are as Real as Those from Alcohol, Tobacco, or Abuse," in *Good Housekeeping,* April 1997, 74.

Bruner quote: Gloria DeGaetano, "Learning from Creative Play," in *Television and the Lives of Our Children* (Redmond: Train of Thought Publishing, 1998), 35.

The most popular children's television shows in 1995 were . . . G. Fabrikant, "The Young and Restless Audience," *The New York Times,* April 18, 1996, D1.

That infants can, and do, imitate an array of adult facial features . . . Brandon Centerwall, "Television and Violence: The Scale of the Problem and Where to Go from Here," *The Journal of the American Medical Association,* vol. 267 (June 10, 1992), 3059.

Emotionally laden images are even more efficient at catching and holding the attention of youngsters . . . Wendy Josephson, *Television Violence: A Review of the Effects on Children of Different Ages.* Ottawa: National Clearinghouse on Family Violence, 1995, 17–19.

. . . case of a preschooler who expressed fear and hostility . . . Wendy Josephson, *Television Violence: A Review of the Effects on Children of Different Ages.* Ottawa: National Clearinghouse on Family Violence, 1995, 19.

. . . but they do not possess an instinct for gauging whether a behavior ought to be imitated: Brandon Centerwall, "Television and Violence: The Scale of the Problem and Where to Go from Here," *The Journal of the American Medical Association,* Vol. 267 (June 10, 1992), 3059.

. . . "they have a refrigerator, and there are such things as refrigerators": H. Kelly, "Reasoning About Realities: Children's Evaluations of Televisions and Books," in H. Kelly and H. Gardner (eds.), *New Directions for Child Development:*

Viewing Children Through Television, no. 13. San Francisco: Jossey-Bass, 1981, 63.

. . . an Indiana school board had to issue an advisory . . . Neal Lawrence, "What's happening to our children?" *Midwest Today,* December 1993.

A seven-year-old boy described a deliberate attempt to reduce his own fear . . . Since identifying with an aggressive hero . . . is chilling indeed: Wendy Josephson, *Television Violence: A Review of the Effects on Children of Different Ages.* Ottawa: National Clearinghouse on Family Violence, 1995, 32.

It has been found that the more unrealistic the character, the more preschoolers both want to be like that character and think they are like that character: D. G. Perry and K. Bussey, "Self-Reinforcement in High and Low Aggressive Boys Following Acts of Aggression," *Child Development,* vol. 48, 1977, 653–657.

. . . young children are more likely to choose fantasy heroes over real-life heroes . . . rather than from friends, siblings, or parents: J. French and S. Pena, "Children's Hero Play of the 20th Century: Changes Resulting From Television's Influence," *Child Study Journal,* vol. 21, 1991, 79–94.

Children with a propensity for violence usually have both learning and behavior problems . . . Gloria DeGaetano, "Cycle Effects from Long-Term Viewing of Television Violence," in G. DeGaetano and K. Bander, *Screen Smarts: A Family Guide to Media Literacy.* Boston: Houghton Mifflin, 1996, 57.

Like 56 percent of kids between ages twelve and seventeen . . . "Television in the Home, The 1997 Survey of Parents and Children," The Annenberg Public Policy Center,

1997, in "TV in the Bedroom," *Better Viewing Magazine,*
September/October 1997, 3.

An estimated four million American children are victimized each
year by physical abuse . . . and other traumatic events:
Ronald Kotulak, *Inside the Brain: Revolutionary Discoveries*
of How the Mind Works. Kansas City: Andrews McMeel
Publishing, 1996, 89.

Research has found that abused children . . . most likely to com-
mit violent crimes later in life: Wendy Josephson, *Television*
Violence: A Review of the Effects on Children of Different
Ages. Ottawa: National Clearinghouse on Family Violence,
1995, 47.

Violent or aggressive people have decreased activity . . . leading
to a short fuse: Two of four characteristics listed by Daniel G.
Amen, M.D., in *Change Your Brain, Change Your Life: The*
Breakthrough Program for Conquering Anxiety, Depression,
Obsessiveness, Anger, and Impulsiveness. New York: Times
Books, 1998, 212.

The brain of the child is not a miniature version of the adult
brain: Florida Starting Points Initiative with support from the
Carnegie Corporation, *Maximizing Washington's Brain*
Power: We Need to Use It or Lose It, October 1997, 7.

In Florida, for instance, a six-year-old boy and his friend . . . Brandon Centerwall, "The TV Message is Mayhem," *Encyclopae-*
dia Britannica: 1995 Medical and Health Annual. Chicago:
Encyclopaedia Brittanica, 1995, 94–95.

When children start off in an alarm state with high noradrenaline
and impulsive behavior . . . revert to low noradrenaline lev-
els and calculating behaviors: Perry, Bruce, M.D., Ph.D.,

"Incubated in Terror: Neurodevelopmental Factors in the 'Cycle of Violence,'" in *Children in a Violent Society,* Joy D. Osofsky, ed. New York: The Guilford Press, 1997, 124–149.

Research indicates that children may be deliberately trying to conquer their fears . . . through repeated exposures to horror movies: D. Zillmann and J. Bryant, "Affect, Mood, and Emotion as Determinants of Selective Exposure," in D. Zillmann and J. Bryant, eds., *Selective Exposure to Communication.* Hillsdale: Lawrence Erlbaum Associates, 1985, 157–190.

Belson study: William Belson, *Television Violence and the Adolescent Boy.* Farnborough, UK: Saxon House, Teakfield Limited, 1978. John P. Murray, "Studying Television Violence: A Research Agenda for the 21st Century," in *Research Paradigms, Television, and Social Behavior,* eds. Joy Asamen and Gordon Berry. Thousand Oaks: Sage Publications, 1998, 387–388.

Constant exposure . . . incapable of producing socially acceptable emotional responses: Paul Gathercoal, "Brain Research and Mediated Experience: An Interpretation of the Implications for Education," *Clearing House,* Vol. 63, February 1990, 271.

The Japanese army very effectively used classical conditioning with their soldiers: Lt. Col. Dave Grossman, "We are training our kids to kill," *Saturday Evening Post,* August 1999, 70.

The conditioning of our children by violent visual entertainment creates an "acquired deficiency" in this immune system. AVIDS . . . Lt. Col. Dave Grossman, *On Killing: The Psychological Cost of Learning to Kill in War and Society.* New York: Little, Brown & Co., 1996, xviii.

We must assume that what we know of the more benign, outdated games of the 1970s . . . *cannot be considered valid for the games that have been put on the market in the last five years:* Eugene Provenzo in *The Social Effects of Electronic Games: An Annotated Bibliography,* eds. Joel Federman, S. Carbone, Helen Chen, and William Munn. Studio City: Mediascope, 1996, ii.

"Globally, annual video game revenues now exceed $18 billion. In the United States alone, video game revenues exceed $10 billion annually, nearly double the amount Americans spend going to the movies. On average, American children who have home game systems play with them about ninety minutes a day": eds. Joel Federman, S. Carbone, Helen Chen, and William Munn, *The Social Effects of Electronic Games: An Annotated Bibliography* (Studio City: Mediascope, 1996), i.

. . . *49 percent of young teens indicate a preference for violent games, while only 2 percent prefer educational ones:* Jeanne B. Funk, "Reevaluating the Impact of Video Games," *Clinical Pediatrics,* vol. 32, no. 2, 1993, 86–90.

Patricia Greenfield quote: Eugene Provenzo, *Video Kids* (Cambridge: Harvard University Press, 1991), 47–48.

More than 60 percent of children report that they play video games longer than they intend to play: Mark D. Griffiths and N. Hunt, "Computer game playing in adolescence: Prevalence and demographic indicators," *Journal of Community and Applied Social Psychology,* vol. 5, 1995, 189–193.

Four basic elements of video games (we have expanded these to make points about violent video games): Jane M. Healy,

Endangered Minds: Why Kids Don't Think and What to Do About It (New York: Simon and Schuster, 1990), 207.

. . . studies show that generally boys' preferences . . . Jeanne B. Funk, "Reevaluating the Impact of Video Games," *Clinical Pediatrics,* vol. 32, no. 2, 1993, 86–90.

For girls . . . associated with lower self-esteem: Jeanne B. Funk, Debra D. Buchman, "Playing Violent Video and Computer Games and Adolescent Self-Concept," *Journal of Communication,* vol. 46, Spring 1996, 19–32.

Study on arcade use among adolescents: Sue Fisher, "Identifying Video Game Addiction in Children and Adolescents," *Addictive Behaviors,* vol. 19, 545–553.

Dr. Donald Shifrin quote: Gloria DeGaetano, personal interview, June 22, 1999.

. . . college students who had played a violent virtual reality game . . . Sandra L. Calvert and Siu-Lan Tan, "Impact of virtual reality on young adults' physiological arousal and aggressive thoughts: Interaction versus observation," *Journal of Applied Developmental Psychology,* vol. no. 5, 1, 125–139.

Mortal Kombat study: Mary E. Ballard and J. Rose Wiest, "Mortal Kombat: The Effects of Violent Video Technology on Males' Hostility and Cardiovascular Responding," March 1995, 8; paper presented at the Biennial Meeting of the Society for Research in Child Development (61st, Indianapolis, Ind., March 30–April 2, 1995).

Soldiers in that war spent a lot of time firing their guns . . . the firing rate was a mere 15 percent among riflemen . . . S. L. A. Marshall, *Men Against Fire.* Gloucester: Peter Smith, 1978, 51.

Their introduction is undeniably responsible for increasing the firing rate from 15 to 20 percent in World War II to 95 percent in Vietnam . . . 75 percent to 80 percent of the killing on the modern battlefield is a direct result of the simulators. Ken Murray, Lt. Col. Dave Grossman, and R. W. Kentridge, "Behavioral Psychology," in *Encyclopedia of Violence, Peace and Conflict.* San Diego: Academic Press, 1999.

Time Crisis brochure quote: Personal correspondence, Jack Thompson and Lt. Col. Dave Grossman, June 1999.

WingMan Force: Advertising copy in *PC Gamer,* cited by President Clinton in his national speech on media violence after the Littleton, Colorado, massacre, June 1, 1999.

Wesley Schafer quote: Lt. Col. Dave Grossman, personal interviews conducted with Wesley Schafer, Union, SC, January 1998.

These two avid video game players fired twenty-seven shots from a range of over one hundred yards, and hit fifteen people: Lt. Col. Dave Grossman, personal interviews conducted with law enforcement officers after the Jonesboro massacre, March 1998.

Description of Duke Nukem game: Media Watch Online: "Duke's the King Baby," www.mediawatch.com.

Gary Eng Walk quote: Gary Eng Walk. "All Gore," *Entertainment Weekly,* Summer Double Issue '99, 143.

Doug Lowenstein quote: Mark Boal. "One Step Ahead of the Law." salon.com, July 19, 1999.

Duke Nukem, rated M for mature audiences, seventeen and older, is shelved next to Eggs of Steel, a kiddie game about an animated egg. Susan Nielsen, "A beginner's guide to becoming a video game prude," *The Seattle Times,* February 21, 1999, B 7–8.

"Fatalities can be the best part of Mortal Kombat," Mortal Kombat action toys are labeled, "For children four and up"; "As easy as killing babies with axes"; "More fun than shooting your neighbor's cat": Susan Nielsen, "A beginner's guide to becoming a video game prude, *The Seattle Times,* February 21, 1999, B 7–8.

Capcom's latest Street Fighter proclaims, "The killer in me is just beginning"; Robert Lindsey quote: "Game Makers Downplay Violent Role," *USA Today,* Internet site (ctc8229.htm at www.usatoday.com), 2.

"The Creators of Redneck Rampage are about to bring you a new, urban drama . . .": "Kingpin: Life of Crime," http//www.interplay.com/kingpin.

CHAPTER 5: DON'T JUST STAND THERE . . . DO SOMETHING!
1998 "State of Children's Television" report: "V-Chip Debuts, Ratings Confuse," *Better Viewing Magazine,* September/October 1998, 3.

Bruce Perry Quote: Perry, Bruce, M.D., Ph.D., "Incubated in Terror: Neurodevelopmental Factors in the 'Cycle of Violence,' " in *Maximizing Washington State's Brain Power.* Olympia: Department of Health and Human Services, Fall 1998, 8.

A recent Canadian study demonstrated that 40 percent of parents . . . A study by Tony Charlton cited by Paul Majendide, "TV Dominates Family Life," *The Seattle Times,* April 1, 1998, E-6.

And an American study has shown that 82 percent of parents . . . do not encourage reading at home: Eric Jensen,

Teaching With the Brain in Mind. Alexandria, Va: Association for Supervision and Curriculum Development, 1998, 23.

Russell Harter quote: Jane M. Healy in *Endangered Minds: Why Kids Don't Think and What to Do About It.* New York: Simon and Schuster, 1990, 208.

"Gratuitous Violence Is 200 Times Faster with a D-Link Network"; "No cure. No hope. Only death"; "Destroying Your Enemies Isn't Enough . . . You Must Devour Their Souls": PC Gamer, vol. 6, no. 8, August 1999. Advertising on pages 142, 104, 22–23.

40 percent of ten- to seventeen-year-olds said they would be less likely to watch such a program. "The Power of Three Hours," *Better Viewing Magazine,* September/October 1997, 3.

Story of Tim: Beverly Robertson Jackson, "Creating a Climate for Healing in a Violent Society," *Young Children,* vol. 52, no. 7 (November 1997), 70.

"21st Century Media Responsibility Act": Mark Boal, "One Step Ahead of the Law," *salon.com,* July 19, 1999.

Mason City, Iowa, has embraced a plan by their mayor to rid the town of violent video game, vowing "zero tolerance" for these murder simulators: "A Ban on Trouble," *Newsweek,* June 14, 1999, 4.

President Clinton quotes: National address by President Clinton, June 1, 1999.

Colorado Attorney General Ken Salazar quote: Ken Salazar, OpEd Column: "Initiatives may arise from dialogue," *Denver Post,* 13 June 1999.

Jack Thompson quote: Personal correspondence, Jack Thompson and Lt. Col. Dave Grossman, June 1999.

In New York, a father taught his eight-year-old how to use and fire a gun . . . Fox News, "Hannity & Colmes," May 12, 1999.

Jennifer James quote: Jennifer James, "Death rattle: last gasp of a failed mind-set," *The Seattle Times,* July 4, 1999, L6.

This is exactly the technique used by some very notable citizens to call for an entertainment industry "Code of Conduct": "An Appeal to Hollywood," www.media-appeal.org.

RESOURCES

A DEFINITION OF MEDIA VIOLENCE

Definition written by authors using the following sources:

Belson, W. *Television Violence and the Adolescent Boy.* Franborough: Teakfield, 1978.

DeGaetano, Gloria, and Kathleen Bander. *Screen Smarts: A Family Guide to Media Literacy.* Boston: Houghton Mifflin, 1996.

Comstock, G., and H. Paik. *Television and the American Child.* San Diego: Academic Press, 1991.

Federman, Joel, ed. *National Television Violence Study, Vol. 3, Executive Summary.* Santa Barbara: University of California, 1998.

Murray, John. "Children and Television Violence," in *Kansas Journal of Law & Public Policy,* 1995, vol. 4, no. 3, pp. 7–14.

VOICES OF CONCERN ABOUT ON-SCREEN VIOLENCE

Information from the American Medical Association: Physician Guide to Media Violence, The American Medical Association, 1996, 4–6.

Information from the American Psychological Association: Violence and Youth: Psychology's Response; vol. 1: Summary Report of the American Psychological Association Commission on Violence and Youth, The American Psychological Association, 1993, 33–35, 77–78.

Information from the American Academy of Pediatrics: "Statement for the Senate Commerce Science and Transportation Committee on the Television Rating System," American Academy of Pediatrics, February 27, 1997.

Information from the National Association for the Education of Young Children: "NAEYC Position Statement on Violence in the Lives of Children," National Association for the Education of Young Children, 1996.

Information from the American Academy of Child and Adolescent Psychiatry: www.aacap.org excerpt used with permission from the American Academy of Child and Adolescent Psychiatry.

Information from the National Parent/Teacher Association: Resolutions used with permission of the National PTA.

A CHRONOLOGY OF MAJOR FINDINGS, STATEMENTS, AND ACTIONS ON MEDIA VIOLENCE, 1952–1999

Adapted from www.videofreedom.com/chrono.html (Original source: Charles S. Clark, *Communication Quarterly*, September 4, 1993).

SELECTED

BIBLIOGRAPHY

Asamen, Joy, and Gordon Berry, eds. *Research Paradigms, Television, and Social Behavior.* Sage Publications, 1998.

Cantor, Joanne. *Mommy, I'm Scared: How TV and Movies Frighten Children and What We Can Do to Protect Them.* Harcourt Brace, 1998.

Carlsson, C., and C. Von Felitzen, eds. *Children and Media Violence: Yearbook from the UNESCO International Clearinghouse on Children and Violence on the Screen.* Nordicom: Goteborg University, 1998.

Condry, John. *The Psychology of Television.* Lawrence Erlbaum Associates Publishers, 1989.

Cress, Joseph, and Burt Berlowe. *Peaceful Parenting in a Violent World.* Perspective Publications, 1995.

Crudele, John, and Richard Erickson. *Making Sense of Adolescence: How to Parent from the Heart.* John Crudele Productions, 1995.

DeGaetano, Gloria. *Media Smarts for Young Folks.* Train of Thought Publishing, 1999.

DeGaetano, Gloria. *Television and the Lives of Our Children.* Train of Thought Publishing, 1998.

DeGaetano, Gloria and K. Bander. *Screen Smarts: A Family Guide to Media Literacy.* Houghton Mifflin, 1996.

Duhon-Sells, Rose, ed. *Dealing with Youth Violence: What Schools and Communities Need to Know.* National Education Services, 1995.

Eron, Leonard, et al. *Reason to Hope: A Psychosocial Perspective on Violence and Youth.* American Psychological Association, 1994.

Federman, Joel. *Television Violence Study,* vol. 3. University of California, 1998.

Fried, Suellen, and Paula Fried. *Bullies and Victims: Helping Your Child Through the Schoolyard Battlefield.* M. Evans and Company, 1996.

Garbarino, James. *Raising Children in a Socially Toxic Environment.* Jossey-Bass Publishers, 1995.

Garbarino, James, et al. *Children in Danger: Coping with the Consequences of Community Violence.* Jossey-Bass Publishers, 1992.

Grossman, Dave. *On Killing: The Psychological Cost of Learning to Kill in War and Society.* Little, Brown & Co, 1996.

Gullotta, T., et al., eds. *Delinquent Violent Youth: Theory and Interventions.* Sage Publications, 1998.

Healy, Jane M. *Endangered Minds: Why Our Kids Don't Think and What to Do About It.* Simon and Schuster, 1991.

Healy, Jane M. *Failure to Connect: How Computers Affect Our Children's Minds—for Better and Worse.* Simon and Schuster, 1998.

Josephson, Wendy. *Television Violence: A Review of the Effects on Children of Different Ages.* Ottawa: National Clearinghouse on Family Violence, 1995.

Kotulak, Ronald. *Inside the Brain: Revolutionary Discoveries of How the Mind Works.* Andrews McMeel Publishing, 1996.

Levin, Diane. *Remote Control Childhood? Combating the Hazards of a Media Culture.* National Association for the Education of Young Children, 1998.

Levin, Diane. *Teaching Young Children in Violent Times: Building a Peaceable Classroom.* Educators for Social Responsibility, 1994.

Levine, James. *Getting Men Involved: Strategies for Early Childhood Programs.* Scholastic, 1994.

Levine, Madeline. *Viewing Violence: How Media Violence Affects Your Child's and Adolescent's Development.* Doubleday, 1996.

Medved, Michael. *Hollywood vs. America: Popular Culture and the War on Traditional Values.* HarperCollins, 1992.

Provenzo, Eugene. *Video Kids.* Harvard University Press, 1991.

Slaby, R. *Early Violence Prevention: Tools for Teaching Young Children.* National Association for the Education of Young Children, 1995.

Walsh, David. *Selling Out America's Children: How America Puts Profits Before Values—and What Parents Can Do.* Fairview Press, 1994.

INDEX

Page numbers in *italics* indicate figures.

abuse. *See* child abuse; domestic violence
Acquired Violence Immune System Deficiency Syndrome (AVIDS), 64
action figures, 39, 51, 53, 80–81
addiction, video game, 68–70
adolescents. *See* teenagers
African-American youth murder victims, 17
age
    American cultural insensitivity to appropriate viewing fare, 34–37
    appropriate television news viewing, 96–97
    movie rating system, 109
    prime years for violent criminal acts, 16
    See also preschoolers; teenagers
aggravated assault. *See* assault
aggression, 7, 133, 134
    brain activity and, *58–64*, 89
    and decreased prefrontal cortex activity, 58
    heroic fantasies of, 55
    studies of increased levels of, 26–32
    video game arousal effects, 70–71
    See also assault rates; violent crime
Allen, Steve, 116
American Academy of Child and Adolescent Psychiatry (AACAP), 127–28
American Academy of Pediatrics, The (AAP), 87, 125–26, 134

American Medical Association, The (AMA), 123–24, 133
American Psychological Association (APA), 124–25, 134–35
Americans for Responsible Television, 147
America Online, 18
animal behavior, 47–48
animal mutilation, 7, 18
anxiety, 35, 36
arcade games. *See* video and computer games
Arkansas. *See* Jonesboro (Ark.) middle school shootings
Army, U.S.
    combat simulator usage, 4–5, 74
    Medical Service Corps, 14
arrest rates
    violent crime, *18, 19*
assault rates, 11, 12, 15
    comparison of murder, assault, and imprisonment (1957–97), *13*
    international per–capita rate increase (1977–93), 10–11
Atrium Society Publications, 147–48
Australia, 10
AVIDS. *See* Acquired Violence Immune System Deficiency Syndrome

Batman movies, 35
behavior problems, 10, 56, 59, 61, 88
Belgium, 10–11
Belson, William, 62
Ben Hur (movie), 85
Bennett, William J., 116

ABOUT THE
AUTHORS

LT. COL DAVE GROSSMAN (U.S.A., RET.) is the author of *On Killing: The Psychological Cost of Learning to Kill in War and Society.* As a West Point psychology professor and professor of military science, Grossman trains medical and health professionals on how to deal with and prevent killing. He trained mental health professionals in the aftermath of the Jonesboro shootings, and has been an expert witness and consultant in several murder cases, including that of Timothy McVeigh and Michael Carneal.

GLORIA DEGAETANO is a nationally recogized educator in the field of media violence, and the author of the critically acclaimed *Screen Smarts: A Family Guide to Media Literacy.*